Brief Psychoanalytic Therapy

Perhaps one of the greatest tasks in the field of psychotherapy is to find a way of retaining the core values of a psychoanalytic attitude within a setting where what can be offered is by its nature limited. There is perhaps no-one else working in the field who has managed so well to maintain this tension than Professor Hobson. This book is a major contribution to the field of mental health. I recommend it to all who work in this area, whether they be counselors, psychotherapists, or psychoanalysts.

Dr David Bell, FRCPsych, Past President of the British Psychoanalytical Society and Consultant Psychiatrist in Psychotherapy, Tavistock and Portman NHS Trust

Can psychoanalytic therapy work in 16 sessions? This fascinating exposition connects what happens between people and what happens inside an individual's mind. Exploring this fundamental connection can lead to profound change. Like a symphony that unfolds from a few basic motifs, this book provides a remarkable insight into how brief psychoanalytic therapy grows from such simple beginnings. The clinical wisdom in this fine book will inspire both beginners and seasoned therapists.

Dr Frank Margison, MD, FRCPsych, Consultant Psychiatrist in Psychotherapy, Gaskell Psychotherapy Centre, Manchester Mental Health and Social Care NHS Trust, and University of Manchester

Stellar autism and child development researcher and Kleinian-leaning psychoanalyst Hobson confirms that style is indeed the man. In this passionate, clearly argued exposition of his version of a "psychoanalytic style of brief psychotherapy," he combines clinical detail with evidence for the distinctiveness of his approach. He distills the essence of psychoanalytic expertise in a 16-session format: the capacity to read and put to therapeutic use the here-and-now transference/countertransference matrix. This book will enrich readers' inner worlds—and words—and reinforce the vitality of time-limed psychoanalytic therapy.

Professor Jeremy Holmes, MD, FRCPsych University of Exeter

Brief Psychoanalytic Therapy

R. Peter Hobson

OXFORD
UNIVERSITY PRESS

Great Clarendon Street, Oxford, OX2 6DP,
United Kingdom

Oxford University Press is a department of the University of Oxford.
It furthers the University's objective of excellence in research, scholarship,
and education by publishing worldwide. Oxford is a registered trade mark of
Oxford University Press in the UK and in certain other countries

First Edition published in 2016

Impression: 1

Published in the United States of America by Oxford University Press
198 Madison Avenue, New York, NY 10016, United States of America

British Library Cataloguing in Publication Data

Data available

Library of Congress Control Number: 2016933114

ISBN 978-0-19-872500-8

Printed and bound by
CPI Group (UK) Ltd, Croydon, CR0 4YY

Oxford University Press makes no representation, express or implied, that the
drug dosages in this book are correct. Readers must therefore always check
the product information and clinical procedures with the most up-to-date
published product information and data sheets provided by the manufacturers
and the most recent codes of conduct and safety regulations. The authors and
the publishers do not accept responsibility or legal liability for any errors in the
text or for the misuse or misapplication of material in this work. Except where
otherwise stated, drug dosages and recommendations are for the non-pregnant
adult who is not breast-feeding

Links to third party websites are provided by Oxford in good faith and
for information only. Oxford disclaims any responsibility for the materials
contained in any third party website referenced in this work.

To Bob and Marjorie, and Jess,
and James, Joe, Amy, and Matthew

Preface

What is psychotherapy? A good question, but not one that is easy to answer. Broadly speaking, psychotherapists take the view that communication within human relationships provides a means through which one person can help another deal with emotional distress and conflict. Beyond this, however, psychotherapists believe in all kinds of things, and practice in all kinds of ways. They differ widely among themselves in how they suppose psychotherapy is best delivered. Most fundamentally, they disagree on how the process of psychotherapy works, and therefore what psychotherapy *is*.

Fortunately, I do not have to bother myself trying to document the myriad manifestations of the talking cure. This book is about a specific form of *psychoanalytic* psychotherapy. Psychoanalytic therapy occupies a modest position within the broader swathe of psychotherapies. Yet even within this restricted province, there are contrasts in practice among clinicians whose common aims are to enable patients to appreciate deeper meanings in their experience, to integrate aspects of their emotional life, to diminish conflict and distress, and to find fulfillment in work, love, and play. I shall be dwelling on one particular style of psychoanalytic work. When I consider alternative ways to conduct psychotherapy, my aim will be to bring out the distinctiveness in what I am trying to describe.

The matter of treatment style will concern me much more than treatment length. This might come as a surprise to those who have heard that psychoanalytic treatment takes years to complete. It will also shock some psychoanalytic colleagues. How on earth could the kinds of development fostered by psychoanalysis take place over a mere 16 sessions? How foolish to imagine that one can circumvent the need for a patient to work through deeply ingrained maladaptive patterns of relationship.

Such skepticism is well founded, and the criticisms well aimed. But it would be premature to allow these concerns to deflect attention from what is at stake. I am not claiming that a brief treatment can achieve all that might be possible in a longer therapeutic engagement. On the contrary, I am sure that in very many instances, it cannot. Rather, I believe that for some patients, a great deal can be accomplished if one adopts a truly psychoanalytic approach within a time-limited framework. Shortly I shall come to what "truly psychoanalytic" means in this context.

I simply do not know for how many patients Brief Psychoanalytic Therapy would be of value. As I shall explain in Chapter 2, there is substantial formal research evidence for the benefits of short-term psychodynamic psychotherapy, and to some degree that evidence is relevant for the therapy I shall be describing. But much remains for future research to establish, perhaps especially about the limitations of the approach. For now, all I can say (and in due course, illustrate) is that through Brief Psychoanalytic Therapy, impressive development and change can take place among a substantial number of patients.

Well actually, that is not all I can say. Of course, measureable symptom relief engendered by any treatment is important. But symptom relief is not everything. In my experience, many people who come to a psychotherapist are hoping to find understanding. They are perplexed and troubled by what they feel and do, or fail to feel and fail to do. They want to be understood, and to understand more about themselves. Often, they are aware that in addition to any "symptoms" they might have—and here I add quotation marks to stress that what counts as a symptom of a medical condition (e.g., the conditions of depression or anxiety) and what counts as a part of the human condition is often moot—they have broader emotional issues to address, and very often difficulties in their relationships. For such individuals, Brief Psychoanalytic Therapy can offer something deeply meaningful and in so doing, all being well, establish foundations for personal growth and development *as well as* symptom relief.

Therefore my emphasis in this book is on the psychoanalytic element of Brief Psychoanalytic Therapy. Much of what is contained in the Treatment Manual of Chapter 5, for example, reflects mainstream psychoanalytic thinking and technique. There is little new here. Not only this, but almost all the principles and clinical techniques are applicable to longer treatments, as well as to those that involve more frequent sessions. As I shall explain in a moment, I am hoping the book might serve as a practice-orientated introduction to *aspects* of psychoanalytic technique as practiced in full psychoanalysis as well as in briefer psychotherapy.

Is this my only reason to have written the book? If so, why does the title suggest I am introducing a new species of treatment, one to add to the bucketful we have already?

Here are some additional reasons. Firstly, throughout Western health services there is a drive toward evolving briefer and less expensive therapeutic interventions. No wonder that within psychotherapy, brief treatments such as Cognitive-Behavioral Therapy (CBT) and Interpersonal Therapy (IPT), each of which has the added appeal of an explicit rationale, a common-sense approach, and research evidence for effectiveness, dominate the scene. These are complemented by brief psychoanalytically informed treatments that include the Conversational Model of psychotherapy (Psychodynamic Interpersonal Therapy, PIT), Cognitive-Analytic Therapy (CAT), and Dynamic Interpersonal Therapy (DIT), each of which occupies a specialist niche within the marketplace. However, to my knowledge there has not been a systematic attempt to explore whether a thoroughgoing psychoanalytic approach can be accommodated within a brief therapy format. If we believe there are people for whom brief treatment is preferable, or if we have no alternative but to offer (or as a patient, to enter) brief psychotherapy, then Brief Psychoanalytic Therapy may constitute a valuable option.

Secondly, I think it is important to represent a psychoanalytic clinical approach in a way that is (a) accessible to a broad audience, including those who dislike jargon and/or who are seeking something practically rather than theoretically orientated, (b) helpful *as an adjunct* to supervised clinical work and theoretical study, for trainees and teachers, and (c) adequate to lay foundations for research. In my view, the essence of psychoanalytic thinking and practice is neither so mysterious, nor so abstruse or even zany, as it is often portrayed. In this book I attempt to distill what I think the essence is, and to make it accessible to all. I am hoping the account might serve as a bulwark, insubstantial though it is, to resist a tide of opinion that threatens to sweep psychoanalytic thinking and practice into a backwater. If psychoanalytic practice is to be given short shrift by the Conventional Wisdom of the Dominant Group (COWDUNG, as pithily characterized by Waddington 1977), then at least this should not be justified on the grounds that there is no clear specification of what it entails.

Having said this, I should stress that what this book offers is not sufficient from either a theoretical or a clinical perspective to enable a clinician to practice Brief Psychoanalytic Therapy. What is required in addition is that the therapist should have a background of relevant psychoanalytic reading and knowledge, substantial experience of supervised work, and a firm grasp of what it means to analyse the transference (of which, more anon).

Finally, I think there is enough distinctive about Brief Psychoanalytic Therapy to justify its having an identity and title of its own. I shall need to make the case for this claim, because it really would not do to peddle an already established treatment under a new name. Moreover, in whatever ways Brief Psychoanalytic Therapy might differ from other treatments, these should matter. Ideally, of course, one would like to provide formal empirical evidence to substantiate the benefits of the approach over and above those of alternative treatments. In the absence of such evidence for this newcomer to the therapeutic scene, I shall offer reasons to think that, along with other psychoanalytically oriented treatments, it may have special power to promote a person's mental development.

I have referred to laying foundations for research. Only once a treatment has become institutionalized in a published manual that distills the nitty-gritty of the clinical approach, does it become available for implementation and evaluation in research settings. Therefore I have produced a succinct description of Brief Psychoanalytic Psychotherapy in the form of a Treatment Manual (Chapter 5). Although this may be considered a pocket guide to clinical work, it is not meant as a teaching manual, nor as a document prescribing what a therapist *should* be doing. Rather, it is intended as a descriptive account of what is characteristic of this particular form of psychoanalytic psychotherapy, and therefore what the treatment will tend to involve.

The Manual does not capture the wide range of interventions or happenings, including periods of quiet listening and/or reflection by a psychotherapist, that will also feature in treatment. A startling omission is that it makes little or no mention of the importance of dwelling on a patient's relationships with family, friends, and colleagues, both past and present, vitally important though such topics are bound to be. Nor does it indicate the huge importance of a therapist's non-verbal communications such as grunts of acknowledgment, spontaneous conjectures, or (providing they are made infrequently and with care) humorous reflections. It would be a sorry psychodynamic treatment that expunged such goings-on. My intention is to help readers appreciate the specialness of one form of psychoanalytic technique by focussing on what is characteristic of the clinical orientation, rather than trying to encompass all that a psychotherapy of this kind would entail.

In this way, then, I hope the book will offer support to trained as well as trainee psychoanalytic psychotherapists who sense that for some patients, worthwhile change may be achieved through the application of psychoanalytic principles even in time-limited treatment. In addition, it provides a springboard for a broader group of clinicians who wish to explore and understand the extraordinary and radical psychotherapeutic approach that we call "working in the transference."

To conclude this Preface, I would like to express my gratitude to patients who have given written consent for me to present anonymized material from their brief psychotherapy. Secondly, I give sincere thanks to colleagues with whom I worked in the Adult Department of the Tavistock Clinic, London, and in particular, those who joined me in a Brief Psychotherapy Workshop. The core group comprised Maxine Dennis, Jo Stubley, Gabriella Rubino, Malika Verma, and myself. We took on and supervised cases, as I got working on the Treatment Manual and Adherence Manual (for which a medical student, Claire Pocklington, helpfully dug out precedents, since at that time I did not know what an Adherence Manual was). The forms of transference interpretation described in the Manual were originally outlined in a paper published in collaboration with Raman Kapur (Hobson and Kapur 2005). Maxine Dennis, Marisa Velazquez, and Andrew Colitz made invaluable contributions to the research described in Chapter 9. The research study involved the cooperation of additional senior colleagues, and would not have been completed but for encouragement and support from the Department's Executive Committee and Director Philip Stokoe. I am hugely indebted to all these individuals, as well as to many other wonderful colleagues in the Adult Department of the Tavistock Clinic.

In this preface, then, I have introduced the idea that even a short-term psychotherapy can be constructed on psychoanalytic principles. I have not said what I mean by this. In Chapter 1, I lay out the psychoanalytic ideas that ground the approach.

Very recently, publications have appeared reporting the conduct of, and results from, the important Tavistock Adult Depression Study (TADS). The design and implementation of this research into longer-term (60 session) psychotherapy for treatment-resistant depression were completed by Tavistock Clinic colleagues and their collaborators, independently of the work described in this book. The fruits of the two undertakings promise to be mutually enriching, for example in offering manuals that afford complementary viewpoints on what psychoanalytic psychotherapy entails (Taylor 2015). The TADS study yielded impressive evidence for the effectiveness of treatment (Fonagy et al. 2015).

interpretation described in the chapter. A paper that was been published by... ...and ...tober 1976 ... ...
Max to Denna Morse ... has... variety... ... ...
contributions to the research... carried on by them. We have each ... involved the conversations (1) ... ... have
been continued for ... discussions with... ... the department's
Executive Committee... ... by individuals... ... as well as... ...
those individuals as well as... from... ... ... in the Adar...
Department of the Institute of...

In this perspective, our... ... ...
cholinergic car... ... ... we... ... ... occupy
what I mean by this. I... ... ...
ground that appears...

... ...
... important series... ... ...
... ...
... ...
... ...
to be... ... ...
... ...
... ... 1974.

Contents

About the Author

Peter Hobson is Emeritus Professor of Developmental Psychopathology in the University of London. He trained as a psychoanalyst at the British Psychoanalytical Society, and is now on faculty at the San Francisco Center for Psychoanalysis. For many years he was a Consultant Psychiatrist in Psychotherapy in the Adult Department of the Tavistock Clinic, London, and in parallel with this, led a research team at the Institute of Child Health, University College, London. He has written two developmentally oriented books, one for academics entitled *Autism and the Development of Mind* (Erlbaum, 1993), and the other a more reader-friendly book that incorporates a psychoanalytic perspective, *The Cradle of Thought* (Pan Macmillan, 2002; Oxford University Press, USA, 2004). He edited and wrote several chapters for a recent book on assessment for dynamic psychotherapy, entitled *Consultations in Psychoanalytic Psychotherapy* (Karnac, 2013).

Chapter 1

The psychoanalytic background

Introduction

It dismays me how much that is spoken, written, and discussed about psychoanalysis is misleading. To some extent, psychoanalysts have brought this on their own heads, not least by couching what they say in unappealing terminology. They have also been guilty of over-stepping the boundaries of what they can explain about the mind and its development. Having said this, there is within psychology and psychiatry surprisingly deep and widespread prejudice as well as ignorance toward psychoanalysis. Psychoanalysis is dismissed as unscientific, disdained as purely subjective speculation, derided as ineffective, and disparaged as a religion (with Freud the supposed Messiah). Some believe it is mainly about sex, others laugh off Freud as a charlatan, yet others think Woody Allen represents all you need to know.

I would not die in a ditch over the scientific status of psychoanalysis. So much depends on what you mean by science, and on the credence you give to the imperialistic claims of the scientific method (or to be more accurate, the array of scientific methods). It may be worth saying that I have spent most of my professional life leading a small team of investigators pursuing scientifically respectable, conventional psychological research in the fields of childhood autism and mother–infant relations (Hobson, 2002/4). In much of that research, we have adopted the methods of experimental psychology. This was reason enough for one eminent research professor to express the view that my interest in and commitment to psychoanalysis *must* be like a religious belief. He could not countenance the possibility that I consider the evidence for many psychoanalytic claims to be as persuasive as the kind of evidence for which he and I share respect.

The therapeutic relationship

The underlying point of contention is: What is to count *as* evidence? The starting point for appraising any route to knowledge is to consider the method through which knowledge is acquired. Of course, psychoanalysis has a method that differs from those employed in other sciences, just as those other scientific methods differ among themselves. The question is whether the psychoanalytic method is as outrageous and undisciplined as its critics would claim, or whether it is appropriate and adequate to deliver truths about the human mind. The matter of making discoveries and of expanding knowledge about how we tick is almost completely separate from another issue with which it is often confused. The second issue is whether psychoanalysis is effective in promoting psychological change and ameliorating emotional disorder and distress.

So what can be said of the evidence that underpins psychoanalytic knowledge, at least by way of introduction? The principal source of evidence is what happens between a patient and psychotherapist in the special conditions created in the consulting room. "What happens" here refers to emotionally infused interpersonal transactions, the kinds of things that go on all the time in our social life. If the patterns of interaction and emotional engagement that take place in psychotherapy did not go on all the time, then what would be the point of giving them such close attention? The effort to understand and articulate what happens in treatment is justified only because what happens in treatment is also what happens in a person's emotional life outside treatment. The curious thing is that however pervasive a given person's patterns of relationship, conflict, and defense may be, very often these escape recognition and understanding *unless* traced out again and again in psychotherapy. Along with this relative obscurity, the patterns of emotional conduct have another property: they tend to repeat themselves *until* recognized and integrated in a new way.

The discovery that people not only repeat patterns of relationship, but also tend to do so in relation to a psychotherapist, is what led Freud to formulate and develop the concept of transference (Freud 1912). The idea here is that under conditions specially created for psychoanalytic treatment, a patient transfers patterns of relatedness and relationship on to the person of the analyst. In his discussion of the case of Dora (Freud, 1905, p. 116), Freud offered this formulation:

> What are transferences? They are new editions or facsimiles of the impulses and phantasies which are aroused and made conscious during the progress of the analysis; but they have this peculiarity, which is characteristic for their species, that they replace some earlier person by the person of the physician.

Although there are far-reaching clinical implications to the fact that transference patterns are rooted in a person's past relationships, including early relationships (Freud's reference to "some earlier person"), the most important thing is that they epitomize a patient's *current* ways of relating to others. In fact they do more than this, because patients' ways of relating to others are intimately connected with their ways of relating to themselves. For example, patients who are harsh in their judgments of other people are very likely to be harsh in their judgments of themselves.

It may be worth emphasizing that often, patients are very partially aware of their underlying expectations or phantasies about other people, and very partially aware of what they do to keep their emotional equilibrium and avoid potential trauma. Yet such psychological goings-on influence many aspects of people's lives, including their intimate relationships, self-esteem, capacity to think, emotional states, affective regulation, and fulfillment in life.

In the course of relating to a therapist in the confiding setting of psychoanalytic psychotherapy, patients experience and re-experience their own particular anxieties, hopes, impulses, and so on, and bring into play their habitual ways of managing emotional challenges and conflicts. In living out critically important patterns of relatedness and defence in the transference relationship with the therapist, they reveal what is most important about themselves, and what most needs to be understood. Potentially at least, both their strengths and difficulties can be registered and recognized as they are expressed. When this happens, there is an opportunity not merely to identify what a patient is doing at that very moment (for instance, keeping things on a polite but superficial level) but also why he or she is doing it (for instance, to avoid underlying rivalry and conflict).

If this seems simple from both theoretical and practical points of view, it is not. As clinical examples in this book testify, it requires a therapist to have emotional sensitivity and skill to identify what is happening in the transference, and it takes emotional work and clinical adroitness to communicate understanding to a patient. In my experience, therapists mean very different things when they claim to work in the transference, and research on what different therapists say to patients reinforces this view (Hobson and Kapur 2005, summarized in Hobson et al. 2013). Then a given therapist needs to select when as well as how to frame interpretations of the transference, and to decide which aspects of a person's state or behavior to address (Riesenberg-Malcolm 1995; Roth 2001; Strachey 1934).

Moreover, understanding is only part of the challenge. A psychotherapist needs to manage how he or she is affected within the therapeutic relationship. Indeed, a therapist's ability to apprehend, understand, deal with, and (sometimes) interpret the transference depends a lot on how the therapist apprehends, understands, and deals with his or her own subjective experience in relation to the patient. This twin focus distinguishes Brief Psychoanalytic Therapy from some other psychodynamic psychotherapies. More than once I shall stress how much study, supervision, and clinical experience is needed to conduct any psychoanalytic therapy, and Brief Psychoanalytic Therapy most of all.

The intersubjective domain

In psychoanalytic psychotherapy, then, a therapist pays very close attention to the ways in which a patient relates to the therapist him/herself. In order to understand the rationale for and practice of psychoanalytic forms of psychotherapy, one needs to appreciate the kind of close attention that applies in this context, and the qualities of patient–therapist relatedness on which attention is focussed. Moreover, the simplicity of the above formulation belies many complexities in relation to the setting for analytic work, the modes of understanding that the analyst brings to bear, and the way he or she communicates with the patient. All this needs to be framed within a developmental perspective and underpinned by a therapeutic rationale that makes sense.

Some features of the setting for Brief Psychoanalytic Therapy are described in the Treatment Manual of Chapter 5. For now, I would emphasize that the psychotherapist is responsible for creating time and space in which the patient has reason to feel safe, even if he or she is unable to trust this fact. The patient should know that the session will be uninterrupted and last for a prescribed length of time (perhaps 50 or 60 minutes, often longer for an assessment consultation), and that the therapist will respect personal boundaries, keep confidentiality, and take responsibility for managing the beginning and end of a session and for giving notice of breaks in treatment. Beyond this, of course, the therapist's obligations include attending to the patient with serious commitment and compassion, and making interventions that promote the patient's development and wellbeing, even when this means that therapist and patient have to experience emotional discomfort. The setting, then, includes both physical and temporal parameters, as well as the psychological availability of the therapist.

What of the mode of understanding that the therapist is seeking to achieve, and that the patient is needing to receive in order to develop and change? The crux is that this is intersubjective in nature. At its most basic, within psychotherapy the therapist has a set of subjective experiences in relation to the patient's subjective experiences, and vice versa. If a patient is angry and openly antagonistic, for instance, the therapist is prone to have corresponding feelings and impulses, perhaps those of being threatened or having an urge to counter-attack. If a patient expresses the pain of loss, the therapist is prone to feel sympathy. From a complementary perspective, if a therapist is clearly thoughtful about what a patient has expressed, the patient may feel relief. In each of these cases, the therapist's and patient's states of mind complement one another (Racker 196). On this level (although in truth, much else would be passing through the minds of each party), the psychological transactions might be conscious.

This description is of intersubjective engagement at its most basic. But even here, there is great significance in the kind of relation that exists between the two human beings in communication with one another. As I have argued elsewhere from a philosophical as well as psychological perspective (e.g., Hobson 1993, drawing especially on Hamlyn 1974), our knowledge of other people as having minds depends upon interpersonal engagement that involves feelings. I shall not rehearse the argument here, but to put it crudely, Martians who could not *feel for and with* human beings would not be in a position to discover that people have their own subjective experiences. Extending this line of thought, our knowledge of *how* people's minds work *also* depends on our capacities to engage with others. Such engagement includes, importantly, our potential to identify with other people's attitudes (e.g., Hobson 2002, 2014). Mostly, we do not observe behavioral cues in a detached way, and then infer mental states. Rather, we engage with a person's mental states as these are expressed through the person's behavior.

In certain respects, intersubjectivity is a long word that captures the obvious. There is little controversial in the claim that in order to feel understood by someone else, one needs to feel that the someone else has a subjectively experienced state in relation to one's own experiences. You don't feel understood by a machine, except perhaps by extrapolating from interpersonal communication. In other respects, however, there is fierce controversy over the status of intersubjective judgments and knowledge.

A principal point of contention is how objective one can be about intersubjective happenings. There are those who insist that what is subjective in terms of that which is personally experienced, is also subjective in being non-objective, idiosyncratic, and non-scientific. And as Hans Eysenck (1985) once expressed the matter, a science cannot be based on subjective interpretations.

Yet this is a flawed argument. Objectivity is the opposite of subjectivity in one sense only. The claim that something is objectively the case is a claim about what is really the case for anyone, and not merely for a given individual who may be mistaken or misguided. From a scientific perspective, objectivity requires that independent observers agree in their judgments over whatever is in question. What is in question can involve intersubjective relations, and in some circumstances one can check whether different people witnessing those relations independently judge them similarly. In the case of interpersonal relations recorded on videotape during psychotherapy consultations, for example, agreements among raters in relevant forms of psychoanalytic judgment are substantial (e.g., Hobson, Patrick, and Valentine 1998).

The intersubjective domain is complicated by three further facts of human psychology. Firstly, not all states that are potentially conscious are present to a person's subjective awareness. Nevertheless, a therapist may find him or herself having emotional responses to a patient's unconscious states and activities of mind. In other words, the intersubjective field extends beyond what is immediately accessible. For example, a therapist might find him or herself wary or even afraid of a patient, when on the surface the patient's communication appears to be polite and matter-of-fact. Or the therapist might sense that despite a patient's seeming helplessness, actually the patient is more in command of himself and what is happening than seems to be the case. The therapist's unconscious is in communication with the patient's unconscious (Bollas 1992; Freud 1923). Often but not always, a therapist's feelings reflect what is going on in the therapeutic relation.

Secondly, not all intersubjective transactions between one person and another have similar qualities of connectedess or sharing. There are a variety of ways in which one person may be affected by the mental state of another. Especially important for psychotherapy are psychological processes of projection and projective identification. Projective identification was first characterized by Melanie Klein (1975a, originally 1946), and is a means by which a patient may induce a therapist to carry some part or parts of what the patient is unable or unwilling to own for him or herself. For example, a patient who is especially vulnerable to humiliation or abandonment might assume a superior attitude to ensure that if anyone is going to be found wanting, or to be left in a needy state, then it is going to be the therapist. Alternatively, a patient who is very meek and passive may provoke the therapist to experience frustration and even sadism corresponding with feelings the patient cannot manage in him or herself. In one sense the feelings induced in the therapist—and these may be hard for the therapist to identify accurately—belong to the therapist, but in another sense they belong to the patient.

How the therapist engages with his or her own feelings in the therapeutic relationship is critical not only for coming to understand the patient, but also for promoting re-integration of what the patient has disowned (see Spillius and O'Shaughnessy 2012 for essays on this topic). The challenge for a therapist is to register, contain and think about these feelings without being scripted into re-enacting something of a patient's habitual patterns of relatedness. An obvious example is that a therapist should beware of responding to an attack with counter-attack. If possible, the therapist will use his or her own experience at such moments as a means to understand the patient's experience and predicament, as well as to recognize the kind of emotional equilibrium the patient is needing to sustain. I shall return to these matters shortly.

The developmental perspective

The third complication, related to the first two, is that the emotional life of human beings follows a developmental trajectory. The maturity and integration of a person's feelings, including feelings of gratitude, concern, regret, and guilt, should not be taken for granted (e.g., Klein 1975b, originally 1957; Winnicott 1965a, originally 1963). If an individual's early development has been compromised, there may be lasting consequences for the person's emotional life. There are a range of ways in which a human being may be restricted in what he or she can feel in relation to other people, but one subtle and profound contrast relevant for much psychoanalytic psychotherapy is between two relational states delineated by Klein (1975a, originally 1946) and called the paranoid-schizoid and depressive positions.

The paranoid-schizoid position is one in which the individual's primary anxieties have to do with threats to the self. Patients in this state are prone to feel that they are being exploited, manipulated, invaded, or subjugated, and that they have to defend their individuality at all costs. They may experience other people not only as persecuting and malign, but also as wonderful and idealized, rather like the wicked and beneficent witches of fairy tales. Their interpersonal relations lack subtlety and flexibility, as well as a sense of mutual respect or concern. These features may be relatively persistent and pervasive in a given person's life, as in some cases of borderline personality disorder (concerning which, see Hobson, Patrick, and Valentine 1998, for a study that provides more clinical detail on the paranoid-schizoid position), or they may be fleeting. Paranoid-schizoid functioning is a potential for us all.

People may assume a very different emotional orientation, one somewhat misleadingly called the depressive position. Patients in the depressive position have anxieties of a different kind. Often their primary concerns are about losing a loved and needed figure, or about causing harm to others. Most important, there is depth and reciprocity to their interpersonal engagement. Human relations, including that with a therapist, entail a sense of potential concern and compassion on both sides. Other people are experienced as persons with their own subjectivity and value. Instead of facing the black-and-whiteness of the paranoid-schizoid world, the person engages with multi-faceted people in relation to whom ambivalent mixtures of love and hate are the norm. Interpersonal relations are deeper, more complex, and more personal.

The implications for clinical technique are profound. First and foremost, one needs to understand how a patient is experiencing the world, internal and external, at any moment in a session, or perhaps in a particular phase of treatment. For instance, it is important not to overlook how threatening and untrustworthy a therapist may feel to someone in the grip of primitive anxieties, and how unsubtle and at times brutal that person's own emotional engagements can be. Secondly, following from this, a therapist needs to adjust his or her communication in accordance with a patient's stance. In the paranoid-schizoid position, for example, a patient may experience a therapist's interpretations of his or her behavior as assaults, and may be unable to think about what the therapist says. It is beyond the scope of this book to explore the variations in therapeutic technique that may be introduced to deal with such challenges (to give but one example, see Steiner 1993 for discussion of patient-centered and analyst-centered interpretations). Shortly I shall consider Bion's (1962a, 1962b, 1967) important idea that a therapist needs to contain a patient's troubled states of mind, but this is easier to describe than to achieve.

The developmental perspective comes in because, according to Kleinian psychoanalytic theory, paranoid-schizoid functioning is a relatively primitive form of social-relational experience, whereas the ability to maintain depressive position functioning is a developmental achievement that depends on an individual having received good enough caregiving early in life. It is not so much that one position precedes or succeeds the other, but rather that they exist in dynamic relation to one another (a matter explored by Ogden 1986). Having said this, a therapist needs to appreciate how development through and beyond paranoid-schizoid functioning has much to do with the receptive understanding and integrative mental work of the therapist.

There is a further perspective to encompass, and this, too, has a developmental dimension. Patterns of interpersonal relatedness occur within the context of longer relationships. After all, there is more than here-and-now relatedness to any relationship. This is self-evident when two people are engaged with each other over time, for instance in a supportive friendship or a drawn-out rivalry, but it is also the case within each individual's mind when they are apart. A toddler will have many different patterns of relatedness toward his or her caregiver, for instance those of neediness or aggressiveness, each of which is anchored in an ongoing attachment relationship. The biological underpinnings and developmental determinants of secure or insecure attachments are not identical with those of attunement in episodes of intersubjective engagement, even though these two levels of social functioning intertwine. Correspondingly, there is scope for mutual enrichment between attachment theory and psychoanalysis over clinical as well as theoretical domains (Fonagy 2001; Holmes 1993).

It is obvious that in psychotherapy, moment-by-moment shifts of interpersonal engagement and relatedness occur in the context of a longer-term relationship between patient and therapist. In psychoanalytic treatment, then, serious attention is given to a patient's evolving relationship with the therapist over time, as well as to events such as breaks and the termination of treatment that challenge a patient's manner of dealing with feelings of mistrust and abandonment or, among more troubled patients, pose existential threats such as the loss of self. These are issues that assume great importance in brief forms of psychoanalytic treatment.

Transference and countertransference

Given the complexities to the intersubjective field between patient and therapist, it is no wonder that psychoanalytic psychotherapists face a challenging task in using their own subjective experiences, and their own unconscious, to evaluate what is happening at any moment in a session. As we have seen, a patient transfers his or her ways of relating to people on to the person of the therapist in the transference, and the therapist is responsive to the roles and feelings induced in him/herself by these very patterns of relatedness, in the countertransference (Heimann 1950; Racker 1968; Sandler 1976). The setting of therapy is intended to create conditions in which the relational patterns to which a patient is disposed become manifest and enacted in the here and now, in such a way that the therapist becomes emotionally implicated. In addition, of course, the therapist's own personality and behavior influence the therapeutic engagement, both affecting the patient's conduct and influencing the therapist's experience of the interaction.

In all of this, then, a therapist's capacity to analyze what is happening through monitoring his or her countertransference is often critical to the success of psychotherapy. The word "monitoring" only partly covers what is involved. I think a more adequate way to describe what happens, is that the therapist needs to relate to his or her own relation with the patient. One example of this is when a therapist catches him or herself being caught up in an exchange with the patient that seems unproductive, or strained, or downright inappropriate, and steps back sufficiently (but not completely) from the therapist's own utterances and feelings to think about how these may reflect something about the patient (Feldman 1997). Perhaps I should add that involvement and recovery are essential to the therapeutic process. A cool, distant and perhaps over-defended therapist is not a good therapist.

In addition, of course, a therapist needs to relate to the patient in a manner that is sensitive and honest. At times this will mean facing unpleasant truths, and not only truths about the patient. The therapist may need to own and privately engage with his or her own destructive impulses or feelings of inadequacy, as these are elicited by a particular patient. The point is that this may be needed if the therapist is to grasp what is happening now, in the session between patient and therapist. Such understanding needs to be contextualized in relation to the patient's current level and quality of functioning, and a view of the processes through which countertransference feelings are being induced. The therapist's aim is not only to discern and take on board the patient's experience of what is happening, and what the patient is needing to communicate or fend off from consciousness, but also to evaluate the patient's ability to be receptive to and to think about anything the therapist may say.

In summary, what the therapist experiences in the countertransference bears an intimate relation to what the patient either feels or would feel if his or her emotional state were not either displaced into the therapist, or otherwise defended against or fragmented. What the therapist comes to know through intersubjective engagement are vitally important things about the patient's functioning, including the degree of depth and coherence to the person's emotional life and the processes through which the patient maintains mental balance. Clearly the therapist experiences what it is like to be *with* this patient, and almost certainly, something of what it is like to *be* the patient. In addition, the therapist may experience what it *would be* like for the patient if current defences were not shaping his or her experience as they are, thereby protecting the patient from conflictual and perhaps unbearable feelings. All this is deeply important for the therapist's work in achieving and communicating therapeutic understanding.

A therapist's function

I have stated that psychoanalytic psychotherapy, including Brief Psychoanalytic Therapy, has the aim of promoting a patient's development. Two questions arise. Firstly, what is the nature of that development? Secondly, how is development to be fostered, and what is the therapist's role in the process?

Neither of these questions is straightforward to answer. The reason is that development is a complex business, and sources of difficulty, deviance, or stagnation in development are correspondingly diverse. However, it is possible to make certain generalizations that apply to nearly all people entering psychotherapy, and others that are relevant for major subgroups of patients.

The place to start is with the transformational power of human understanding. Human beings need to feel understood (Britton 1998). Expressions of understanding take various forms, from the sensitive nurturing care of a parent toward an infant, to a therapist's linguistically expressed understanding of a patient. To repeat something that is more or less obvious, interpersonal understanding is an emotional and relational business. Words are not enough. This is self-evident in caregiver–infant relations and no less true for therapeutic relationships.

I have noted that one way in which psychoanalysts capture a critical dimension of this form of understanding is to talk of a therapist's containing function. This roughly corresponds with an everyday meaning of "contain," as when one says that someone cannot contain his grief, excitement, or whatever. It goes beyond such meaning in two essential respects. Firstly, it applies to what happens between two (or more) people. One person can contain another's emotional state. Institutions, too, may function to contain disturbance.

Secondly, the psychoanalytic notion of containment is often but not always embedded in a particular theoretical orientation to certain forms of interpersonal communication. This theoretical stance originates in the work of Klein (1975a, originally 1946) and especially Bion (1959, 1962a, 1962b). The central idea (well elaborated from a philosopher's perspective by Wollheim 1969) is that a person may treat mental states such as feelings as if they had properties akin to physical things. As I described earlier, a person may locate certain states or feelings beyond the boundary of his or her own personal experience in someone else. In fact, of course, this is a phantasy, because the feelings still belong to the patient. For this reason, some analysts (e.g., Sandler and Rosenblatt 1987, originally 1962) insist that the person locates the feelings in a mental representation of the other person. In any case, most psychoanalysts agree that often but not always, whatever happens is not simply a redistribution of mental states across boundaries that exist within an individual's own mind, because there is also an effect on the therapist (here Sandler 1976 writes of the therapist's role-responsiveness). Not infrequently, the therapist comes to feel, as part of his or her own experience, that which the patient has projected.

A patient might have a variety of motives for locating mental states in a psychotherapist through processes of projective identification (Rosenfeld 1988, originally 1971). Three of these are especially important. One is to communicate something significant *to* the therapist, often by getting under the latter's skin. A second is to get rid of feelings that the individual cannot tolerate or manage. A third is to control the mind of the therapist, in some cases to deny separateness. In each case, if the psychotherapist can register, assimilate, and contain the projected feelings, then the patient may take into him/herself an experience of his/her own unmanageable feelings being managed (Bion 1962a), and thereby acquire new abilities to deal with those feeling for him/herself.

This general development principle can apply in rather different ways to different therapeutic circumstances. A therapist's understanding, including understanding of what is being projected, can enable patients to recognize and tolerate what they have been disowning, and integrate feelings and parts of themselves that had been split asunder. As the case vignettes in this book illustrate, this can be more or less difficult to achieve even with patients who have relatively balanced emotional lives. By and large with these patients, the task is to help the patient tolerate and recognize relational states that are already half-known and familiar, for instance those involving jealousy, rivalry, hatred, or vulnerability. Once identified and acknowledged, they make sense as part of the person's emotional repertoire.

With more troubled patients, what is split off from conscious awareness may be more difficult for the person to re-integrate. One reason is that in these cases, the forces tending toward fragmentation are stronger, and the person's psychological states may be segregated into widely separated black and white portions, or worse still, dispersed in bits and pieces that are not amenable to thinking (Bion 1962a). The pain and conflict that comes with integrating and thinking about disturbing, and perhaps violent, feelings may be just too difficult to bear. Yet even here, development toward more integrated functioning may be promoted by a therapist's capacity to assimilate, think about, and make sense of what cannot yet be thought about by the patient alone.

I should add that this critical matter of a therapist making sense of emotional engagement with a patient may be conceptualized in various ways, not all of which pivot on the notion of projective identification. The central importance of a therapist's emotional availability and capacity for reflection transcends any given theoretical account of the mechanisms by which transference and countertransference are generated.

Having said this, it is important to become familiar with the intrapsychic and interpersonal means by which different patients configure their emotional lives. Just as there are different ways to evade psychic pain and conflict, so, too, there are diverse pressures that may be brought to bear on a therapist as patients attempt to evade or distort their psychological realities. Perverse patients may enlist sexual excitement to obscure their destructiveness as well as emptiness; psychopathic patients may bamboozle the therapist as well as themselves with charm and deviousness; narcissistic patients may elevate and idealize aspects of themselves and repudiate dependency; and so on. Many patients attempt to recruit the therapist in reinforcing, rather than challenging, their emotional *status quo*. Each circumstance will tax the therapist's ability to reflect on whatever he or she feels to be happening in the transference and countertransference. The therapist will need to confront the truth with the patient in whatever way, and to whatever degree, the patient can tolerate. If a therapist can sort out what he or she feels in the countertransference, and think about and then articulate, rather than be overwhelmed by (or reflexly reactive to), what a patient communicates, then this provides an invaluable basis for understanding the patient and making sensitive and incisive interventions.

Here, then, are the clinical and theoretical foundations upon which Brief Psychoanalytic Therapy is built. There is a deceptive simplicity in my description. What is easy to appreciate in outline is often very difficult to apply in reality. Any psychotherapist intending to adopt this therapeutic approach will require intensive training and supervision. This is especially true when psychoanalytic psychotherapy is to be conducted over a brief span of time, because the therapist needs to pick up and address, often with confidence and firmness. patterns of patient–therapist relatedness that emerge in the transference. In order to do so, the therapist will require a capacity for receptiveness toward a patient that is often difficult to achieve and sustain, especially in the heat of the therapeutic encounter.

Nevertheless, the challenges are not insuperable for potentially committed and sensitive clinicians, and the process of becoming a psychoanalytic psychotherapist can prove deeply rewarding. I hope that through specifying and illustrating a psychoanalytic approach compatible with brief psychotherapy, this book might help readers to see how certain principles of analyzing and interpreting the transference are exemplified in practice. One of my aims is to provide an entry-point for a relative novice to learn more about a psychoanalytic stance in terms that are neither esoteric nor bewildering. From a complementary perspective, this book may lend support to clinicians who are already skilled in psychoanalytic psychotherapy but who have shied away from applying their skills to helping people for whom brief therapy is a sole option.

What's missing?

This introduction, indeed this whole book, takes the reader only so far. Several times I have broken off my account when more elaboration was needed, and indicated how readers who are fresh to psychoanalytic ideas might need to combine study of the literature with supervision for their clinical practice. True, I have given prominence to themes that are to the fore in current psychoanalytic thinking. But of course, there are many psychoanalytic concerns, both past and present, that I have not considered. What of the structure of primitive unconscious (primary process) thinking, for example, not to mention the forms of symbolizing that this often entails (Freud 1915; Rycroft 1968, originally 1956). What of the nature of unconscious phantasy, not merely as the backcloth to experience but also as a means by which defensive processes are effected (Isaacs 1948)? What of the importance of triangular relations, including the Oedipus complex, not just for a person's tolerance of other people's relations with third parties, but also for the ability to move among alternative positions within their own minds (Britton, Feldman, and O'Shaughnessy 1989)? What of the status and implications of unrepresented mental states (Botella and Botella 2005; Levine 2012)? On these and other matters, I shall merely state that they amount to perspectives that enrich and deepen psychoanalytic work. Anyone would be better placed to practice Brief Psychoanalytic Therapy if they could draw on these intellectual resources. Whether having appreciation of such perspectives is necessary for conducting this form of therapy is a matter I leave open.

What I do need to stress, and stress repeatedly, is that neither therapeutic technique nor familiarity with analytic literature is enough. Technique and theory are means to an end. However much this book is orientated to technique, technique is merely a vehicle through which a therapist facilitates a patient's development. One aim of technique is to help a patient reveal and explore his or her mental life, and to do so by drawing on the emotional resources of the therapist. Through the therapist's understanding and containment, and through the therapist communicating that understanding and containment by means of an emotional stance that is often conveyed through words that give form to feelings—through all this, all being well, a patient becomes able to integrate what had previously been unintegrated. What matters most is the special kind of interpersonal engagement and communication that a psychotherapist offers.

Therefore technique and theory are of value for clinical work only insofar as they promote sensitive interpersonal exploration and communication. Each is supposed to enhance a therapist's capacity to *listen with feeling*, to foster conditions in which more becomes available to be heard and felt, and to support a therapist's efforts to convey understanding. They are supposed to enrich and facilitate communication between patient and therapist. If instead, technique and theory become barriers to such personal receptiveness and engagement, then something has gone seriously wrong.

Chapter 2

Themes and variations in brief psychodynamic psychotherapy

Introduction

Having outlined the psychoanalytic thinking that underpins Brief Psychoanalytic Therapy, I turn to how psychodynamic principles are applied in a range of brief treatments and begin to explore how far the present approach is or is not distinctive. I should stress that this matters not because Brief Psychoanalytic Therapy needs independent status as a recognized player in the league of dynamic therapies. If it turns out to have a near-identical therapy twin, then hopefully the contents of this book will contribute to explicating aspects of that similar treatment approach. There is no need for a turf war over names, because what matters is the way in which psychotherapy is practised.

The important question for any psychotherapeutic treatment is whether something distinctive in therapeutic orientation and technique needs to be documented and understood for its potential value in enhancing patients' well-being. Therefore the critical issue for Brief Psychoanalytic Therapy is whether it embodies a mode of interpersonal communication and understanding that has special relevance and power for promoting certain forms of personal development.

At the outset, it is worth asking whether any *brief* psychodynamic psycho-therapy makes sense. Brevity is a relative term, and some would consider a treatment of, say, 16 sessions, lengthy and even self-indulgent. However, this is substantially more condensed than longer-term forms of psychotherapy that last for over a year, and each of the treatments I shall describe shortly would be deemed short-term in nature. So the issue is whether the kinds of personal problem that any given mode of psychotherapy is designed to tackle can really be characterized, addressed, and changed in so short a time.

There is good reason to have doubts about this. After all, there will be much to discover that is personal to particular patients, and a complex web of factors from the past and present to negotiate. Beyond this, and at least as importantly, most human beings are resistant to change. People have a natural inclination to hold fast to customary ways of dealing with emotional conflict and distress. In view of this, surely, 16 sessions are but a drop in a lifetime's ocean.

My response to this important question is that we shall have to see. Short-term and longer-term treatments are not the same. What matters is whether, even over a brief span of time, valuable psychodynamic work can be done in a way that is meaningful, coherent, and of lasting value for the patient.

A second question arises. In order to make brief psychodynamic therapy meaningful, coherent, and of lasting value, how does a psycho*analytic* approach have to be shaped or modified? To many, it seems obvious that in order to use limited therapeutic time to best effect, one needs to alter the structure of classic forms of psychoanalytic psychotherapy. Among the most important modifications advocated are that a therapist should be more direct and even directive, giving advice or instruction where necessary, and that there should be an explicitly formulated and consistent focus on which to work, sometimes supplemented by a further written formulation for patients to take with them at the end of treatment. These adjustments in technique seem sensible. And yet … under what circumstances and for what purposes are they needed and/or well advised, and how might they be unhelpful?

In order to frame a context within which this question can be addressed, I shall provide a synoptic overview of five well-known versions of short-term individual psychotherapy. Of course this is a modest sample from a wide array of brief psychodynamic psychotherapies, some of which (e.g., Brief Relational Therapy as described by Safran 2002) might be seen as cousins to the sixth approach I shall summarize, Brief Psychoanalytic Therapy. I am aware that a terse description of intervention strategies leaves out what is often most important, and most characteristic, of a particular approach, namely *how* a therapist and patient engage with one another on a personal-cum-professional level. Therefore I shall add short and not fully representative samples of patient–therapist verbal exchanges from each treatment, just to give a flavor of what they are like in practice. Readers who are interested in particular forms of psychotherapy would do well to consult longer case descriptions that include verbatim clinical material. In the case of Brief Psychoanalytic Therapy, such fine-grained clinical accounts appear in the chapters that follow.

For purposes of the present chapter, then, I shall outline qualities that characterize six forms of treatment. Partly because expressions such as IPT and CAT are common currency among psychotherapists, and partly for ease of presentation, I shall employ acronyms where this seems appropriate. The question arises: what about an acronym for Brief Psychoanalytic Therapy (to which I have already given capital first letters)? I am ambivalent about this, partly for aesthetic reasons and partly because I am reluctant to confer "it-ness" on an orientation that, *in part*, I see as a style of therapeutic work rather than a stand-alone form of treatment. On the other hand, a concrete, highly specified category of treatment is exactly what is needed for conducting research. A sharply delineated and constrained mode of therapy also has value as a kind of prototype, exemplifying certain principles in relatively pure form. Not only this, but also there is much to be said for applying these principles in a consistent and persistent manner over the course of therapy, rather than adding them in as one ingredient in an eclectic mix of procedures. In these respects, a formal title and perhaps an acronym are appropriate.

A final consideration bears on the question of "What's in an acronym?" Brief Psychoanalytic Therapy is just one *particular* way of conducting "brief psychoanalytic therapy." My capital letters are intended to highlight this tight focus and restricted claim. Paradoxically, to give a treatment an acronym, even more than capital letters, is to acknowledge its limited scope. No-one should suppose that the therapeutic work recounted in this book represents the only or quintessential way of applying psychoanalytic principles in brief therapy, nor *a fortiori*, that it distils or integrates "best practice" from a range of approaches.

Therefore on this matter, I have arrived at an uneasy compromise: I shall use the acronym BPT, when indicated, in three domains: (1) the remainder of this chapter; (2) in Chapter 9, on research; and (3) when making reference to the BPT Manual and Adherence Manual, each of which applies to the closely defined, circumscribed version of treatment.

In what follows I describe one approach, Interpersonal Therapy (IPT), that is only marginally psychodynamic. This is included for the reason that it features in research to be described later in this book (Chapter 9). The remaining forms of brief psychodynamic therapy will be Cognitive-Analytic Therapy (CAT), Dynamic Interpersonal Therapy (DIT), Intensive Short-Term Dynamic Psychotherapy (ISTDP), the Conversational Model (a version of which became known as Psychodynamic Interpersonal Therapy, or PIT), and Brief Psychoanalytic Therapy (BPT). I myself have practiced only the last treatment on this list, so for the others I shall be drawing on descriptions from the literature rather than first-hand experience. I shall try to do justice to the principles of each, even if I cannot write about their clinical strengths and shortcomings. In what follows, I would encourage readers to imagine what it is like to engage *as a patient* in each form of psychotherapy.

Interpersonal Therapy (IPT)

Background and aims

The following excerpt from Weissman, Markowitz, and Klerman (2007, p. 68) conveys the orientation of IPT:

> The therapist is the patient's advocate … trying to understand things from the patients' point of view and validating it (aside from the depressive outlook), siding with them against a sometimes hostile environment and encouraging them to do things that they are capable of doing to change that environment … The patient's expectations of assistance and understanding from the therapist are realistic and are not to be interpreted as a reenactment of the patient's previous relationships with others. The assistance that IPT therapists offer is limited to helping patients to learn and test new ways of thinking about themselves and their social roles and solving interpersonal problems.

This last statement, with its emphasis on "helping patients to learn and test new ways of thinking," points to the kinds of developmental process envisaged to underlie change.

Therapeutic approach

The IPT therapist instils hope in and actively supports the patient by encouraging a balance between joint and independent work. He or she maintains an expectation of change, and reinforces the view that IPT is effective treatment for depression and that the patient is expected to take an active role in changing. The therapist links affect as well as changes in affect to interpersonal events/relationships, and uses clarification, summarizing and feedback to stress the importance of interpersonal events/relationships for depression. The therapist attempts to maintain a focus, and redirects the patient's attention if he or she moves away for too long.

Initial sessions exemplify the approach, and include the following:

- a thorough exploration of symptoms of depression
- developing a clear picture of current and past episodes
- explaining the diagnosis and the effectiveness of treatment
- constructing an interpersonal inventory through a thorough exploration of important relationships, with particular attention to expectations and dis/satisfaction
- formulating the presenting problems within an interpersonal frame.

The formulation leads to identifying and agreeing upon a focal area of work. Mid-phase sessions start with a review of symptoms of depression, which are

are linked to the chosen focal area. In the termination phase, progress in the treatment is reviewed.

Here is one example of the kind of exchange that occurs in IPT. This is an excerpt from a longer transcript given by Weissman, Markowitz, and Klerman, 2007, p. 121, concerning therapy with someone who had chronic depression:

D (PATIENT): So, I guess I should talk to Jack about his helping with Kayla, but it's not going to work.

THERAPIST: What would you want him to do? What would be helpful to you?

D: I'd like him to really understand how hard it can be to live with her. He's never home, and when he is, the kids are my responsibility ... It's my fault for not bringing her up better; that's why she's having these problems. I know we've discussed that I blame myself because I'm depressed, but he blames me, too.

THERAPIST: Do you agree? Is that fair?

D: Sometimes I get confused. But no, I guess I more and more don't think it's fair. The psychologists say that we didn't do anything wrong to Kayla.

THERAPIST: So how do you feel when Jack blames you?

Overall, the IPT therapist and patient work alongside one another in a collaborative effort to examine the patient's difficulties in an interpersonal framework.

Cognitive Analytic Therapy (CAT)

Background and aims

Cognitive analytic therapy was developed by Anthony Ryle (see Ryle and Kerr 2002 for a comprehensive overview), and as its name implies, draws on both cognitive therapy (for instance, in goal setting) and analytic psychotherapy (for instance, in its focus on interpersonal role relationships). The aim of the treatment is to enable a patient to recognize and modify patterns of maladaptive behavior, in part by understanding their origins. There is a strong educational bias, insofar as a major aim is to introduce patients to fresh ways of thinking about, and dealing with, their own feelings and conduct. The therapist is explicit about this being a collaborative enterprise, and offers theoretical "scaffolding" to enhance self-reflection. At the same time, the therapist may draw attention to ways in which a patient's characteristic ways of experiencing and dealing with relationships are relevant for understanding patient–therapist transactions during psychotherapy itself.

Therapeutic approach

A CAT therapist begins by taking a history that includes an account of present-day problems and early life experiences. The patient may be given homework in the form of a questionnaire, to fill out further details. On this basis, a list of target problems are formulated in collaboration with the patient, who may be asked to keep a diary to track how the problems are elicited and perpetuated. During this initial phase, patient and therapist work together to arrive at a perspective on the patient's repeating maladaptive patterns of behavior.

Building on these foundations, the therapist writes a "reformulation" letter to the patient which sets the problems in developmental perspective. It clarifies both the procedural sequences that the patient employs (with a focus on self-perpetuating cycles or "traps" in unfulfilling goal-directed activity, and false or restricted options called "dilemmas," and "snags" that prevent potentially valuable courses of action reaching completion) and the role-relationships that the patient tends to experience and/or create.

In subsequent sessions, the patient comes to recognize these patterns in everyday life and in sessions, and can try out alternative ways to respond. Sometimes the therapist supports change not only by encouragement, but also through active role-play. The termination of treatment is discussed, and as this approaches, the therapist gives the patient a goodbye letter, recapping how the patient came to therapy and what has or has not been achieved. Often there is a follow-up appointment after about three months.

Here is a very brief and partial excerpt of a transcript from Introducing Cognitive Analytic Therapy, by Ryle and Kerr (2002, p. 193):

SAM (PATIENT): … I'll give you an example: I can see a plane crash on TV or kids starving and it doesn't touch me—things that should mean something. But to us it don't mean a thing …

THERAPIST: Isn't that because from a very early age you learnt to cut off from painful feelings because they were so overwhelming …

SAM: Oh yeah, so now it's automatic.

THERAPIST: Are you saying that because you can do that then it makes you bad?

SAM: Yeah, I'd go along with that, yeah.

THERAPIST: Well I don't think that makes you evil; It's how you learned to survive as a kid and it still happens. But I don't think it makes you bad.

SAM: Well we do. (pause)

THERAPIST: But I can see where you are coming from. (pointing to the [CAT] diagram) Abusing, attacking yourself. (pause). Thinking about—In the letter to your stepfather, I was struck by where you wrote how he never gave you any affection.

As Denman (2001, pp. 249–250) summarizes in a helpful overview, "CAT shares with cognitive therapy a stress on the detailed analysis of the conscious antecedents and consequences of symptoms, the production and sharing of a detailed descriptive formulation with the patient, the setting of homework and a focus on, and problem-solving approach to, difficulties." In its sensitivity to aspects of transference and countertransference, however, and more generally in its concern with reciprocal role relationships and their developmental significance for a patient's problems and for therapy, it has a psychodynamic dimension.

Dynamic Interpersonal Therapy (DIT)

Background and aims

Here Lemma, Target, and Fonagy (2010, pp. 329, 331, and 333, respectively) offer a good summary: "DIT is based on a distillation of the evidence-based brief psychoanalytic/psychodynamic treatments pooled together from manualized approaches that were reviewed as part of the competence framework for psychological therapies … DIT deliberately uses methods taken from across the board of dynamic therapies," and represents "an opportunity to develop a protocol that integrated core, shared analytic principles and techniques grounded in the extant evidence base."

The DIT therapist has two aims:

1. To help the patient understand the connection between his presenting symptoms and what is happening in his relationships by identifying a core, unconscious, repetitive pattern of relating that becomes the focus of the therapy.
2. To encourage the patient to reflect on his own states of mind and so enhance his ability to manage interpersonal difficulties.

The developmental perspective is one in which "DIT primarily targets the capacity to think about and understand changes in mood symptoms and interpersonal functioning" (Lemma et al. 2010, p. 337).

Therapeutic approach.

There are five relatively simple strategic steps in the course of a brief therapeutic engagement (Lemma et al. 2010, pp. 333–334):

1. Identify an attachment-related problem with a specific relational emotional focus that is felt by the patient to be currently making them feel depressed.

2. Work with the patient collaboratively to create an increasingly mentalized picture of interpersonal issues raised by the problem.
3. Encourage the patient to explore the possibility of alternative ways of feeling and thinking ... actively using the transference relationship to bring to the fore the patient's characteristic ways of relating.
4. Ensure the therapeutic process (of change in self) is reflected on.
5. Near the end of treatment present the client with a written summary of the collaboratively created view of the person and the selected area of unconscious conflict ... to reduce the risk of relapse.

Here one can see how:

> DIT draws liberally on supportive and expressive techniques while also making judicious use of directive techniques to support change within a brief time-frame ... This greater activity does not usually involve giving advice, but it requires that the therapist is alert to any deviations from the agreed focus so as to re-direct the patient back to the focus.
>
> (Lemma et al. 2010, pp. 340–341)

I find it impossible to convey in a single excerpt what earlier I described as "a flavour" of DIT, for the reason that it seems to comprise disparate elements. Therefore let me cite two contrasting passages of clinical description from *Brief Dynamic Interpersonal Therapy* by Lemma, Target, and Fonagy (2011). Here the authors emphasize how interpreting the transference relationship is principally a means *"to enhance the exploration of the IPAF"* (p. 175, original authors' italics, where an IPAF is a preformulated interpersonal-affective focus), and involves "a more explicit effort to help the patient to eventually extrapolate from the transference to his external world of relationships so as to support attempts at new ways of relating" (p. 179). I emphasize these points, because in other respects, the following exchange might represent the kind of transference-focussed work to which a BPT therapist aspires. Here is the excerpt from Lemma et al. (2011, pp. 179–80):

T (THERAPIST): I think it would be helpful if we pause for a minute to look at what has just been happening here between us, because it seems to me that you are feeling rather despairing and hopeless about whether coming here can be of any help to you, and your anxiety does seem to be getting worse, and yet you are not communicating directly to me. Instead I feel you withdrawing. We know how difficult it is for you to be in the position of feeling that you are on your own with a problem and that the other person cannot help you with it. This often leaves you feeling angry, but instead of expressing what you feel you shut down communication. This is similar to what happens with your husband when you get into a conflict with him, just as you were describing to me earlier on in the session.

PT (PATIENT): I know. I do that. I don't feel able to change this. I don't seem able to communicate normally with others. It must be frustrating for you …

T: What is difficult here is that you pull away instead of us being able to think together about how you are feeling worse and how you feel the therapy is not helping. The risk then is that you might just not come back, that you might disappear …

PT [sounds taken aback]: I have been thinking about whether it's worth continuing with this … I hadn't wanted to tell you though in case you thought I was being difficult.

T: So it's safer not to tell me, but this also then means that there is no possibility for us to work out a way forwards.

In DIT, if I understand correctly, episodes of sensitive interpretive work such as this are nested among other, very different styles of intervention. This can be illustrated through a second excerpt that the authors use to indicate what a therapist might say as a "directive intervention" (p. 167):

> You feel very stuck and you are clearly telling me this is causing you a lot of distress. The more you avoid talking with your partner about what's on your mind, the more you withdraw into yourself and then the more depressed you seem to feel. If you could replay this exchange what do you think you might do differently?

From my limited reading about DIT, I derive a mixed picture. At times we see a therapist devoted to the exploration of meanings in the therapeutic relationship, at other times the therapist and patient appear to be engaged in joint tasks akin to those of constructing a relationship schema, or in more specific kinds of problem-solving.

Intensive Short-Term Dynamic Psychotherapy (ISTDP)

Background and aims

Malan and Della Selva (2006, Chapter 2) describe how Davanloo (e.g., 1994, originally 1978) drew heavily on psychoanalytic theory in "creating techniques designed to identify and remove defences against emotional closeness" (Malan and Della Selva, 2006, p. 15). Such defences may be motivated by a range of conflictual feelings such as anger and accompanying guilt over the pain and grief of traumata associated with attachment relationships. Self-punitive attitudes may complicate the picture. Of course, issues such as these have received close attention in the psychoanalytic literature.

Davanloo's particular contribution has been to suggest quite how a therapist should confront a patient's defences against his or her true feelings as these arise in psychotherapy. The aim is to "unlock the unconscious" and enable the patient to experience directly what had been avoided. Once feelings toward the therapist are experienced, patients tend to make connections with important relationships in the past, and traumatic events can be worked over afresh. In the course of this process, interpretations may be used to consolidate insights obtained through emotionally felt experience.

Therapeutic approach

The following is a condensed account of the basic techniques of ISTDP, drawn largely from Malan and Della Selva (2006). As these authors explain (p. 19):

> The ISTDP therapist takes an uncompromising stance as an advocate for the patient and his freedom. The therapist communicates the utmost care and respect for the patient as a human being, while maintaining an attitude of disrespect and intolerance for the defences that cripple the patient's functioning and perpetuate his suffering.

Malan and Della Selva (2006, pp. 19–20) summarize the "central dynamic sequence" of ISTDP in a series of points that I have shortened and somewhat modified in what follows. In brief, the therapist tends to:

1. Begin with an initial enquiry about the patient's complaints.
2. Exert pressure toward the patient experiencing feelings in relation to other people, including the therapist, and focus on sources of anxiety.
3. Identify and clarify defences (e.g., "Do you notice you are vague?," "Do you see that by remaining vague you avoid your feelings?"), and examine their consequences ("If you continue to avoid your feelings by remaining vague, we will not get to the bottom of your problems").
4. Address defences so there is a breakthrough of feelings, or a crystallization of resistance to the process of psychotherapy—in which case, manage a "head-on collision" in which the therapist points out that maintaining the defensive wall against meaningful contact will destroy the opportunity for receiving help. "In some cases, the therapist must confront the patient with the futility of continuing in this manner, suggesting that they will have to say their goodbyes unless these tactics are abandoned" (Malan and Della Selva, p.26).
5. Attend to the breakthrough of complex feelings toward significant others from the past.
6. Offer interpretations to link past and present relationships, including that with the therapist, to consolidate insights.

Throughout, the therapist tries to strengthen the patient's conscious will to join with the therapist in addressing the work in hand.

Here is an exchange taken from Davanloo's work (Davanloo, 1994, originally 1978, pp. 256–257), between Davanloo as therapist and someone characterized as an "angry, childlike woman":

T (THERAPIST): Is there any time that you felt so depressed that you wanted to do away with yourself, that you felt there was no sense in living and wanted to terminate your life?

PT (PATIENT): No. At times I feel doomed. Sometimes I think I want to kill myself, but I think about my children and how horrible it would be for them.

T: You feel you want to do away with yourself, but then you think about the children?

PT: Yes.

T: Right now, how do you feel?

PT: I feel sad.

T: Do you feel like crying?

PT: Yes.

T: I question that because I felt a few times you wanted to cry here.

PT: Yes.

T: But then somehow you went dry, let's say.

PT: It's sort of a waste of time to cry. I'd rather talk.

T: In other words, you feel talking is more important then your feelings?

PT: Yes.

T: And this is a problem, isn't it, that you give priority to talking rather than to the way you feel?

PT: Yes

T: Has it always been like this?

PT: Yes.

T: Do you feel lonely in life?

PT: Often I do, yes.

T: As if in a way you don't really belong? [here the patient agrees, and the therapist makes links with the patient's childhood experiences].

Or again, here is an example of a therapist's intervention, from Malan and Della Selva 2006, p. 31:

> So, do we agree, then, that a big part of the problem for you is in letting yourself feel your anger as anger and using it to assert yourself, instead of going to a weepy, helpless state and turning it back on yourself?

These quotations illustrate the therapist's manner of exploring the emotional dimension of a patient's experience, as well as the educational slant to ISTDP.

The Conversational Model (Psychodynamic Interpersonal Therapy, PIT)

Background and aims

Dr. Robert Hobson (my father, known to colleagues, students and almost everyone else as Bob Hobson) developed what he called the Conversational Model of psychotherapy. This was in the context his experience as a Jungian analyst as well as a psychotherapist within the UK National Health Service, where for a long time he was responsible for an in-patient ward run on therapeutic community lines. In his book, *Forms of Feeling* (R.F. Hobson 1985, from which all subsequent page-numbered quotations are taken), Bob Hobson lays out the theoretical basis for his approach in chapters with headings such as Persons, Symbols, and Seeing. The theoretical orientation he adopts is strongly influenced by writings in philosophy and literature, perhaps most notably those of Buber, Wittgenstein, and Coleridge.

About half way through his book, Bob Hobson summarizes the thinking behind and procedures of the Conversational Model. In part from a wish to provide explicit guidance for would-be psychotherapists at the very beginning of their training, and in part because he believed there are some simple but valuable ways to foster engagement with someone at an emotionally deep level, Bob Hobson listed certain principles that might shape a therapist's interventions. His further aim was to specify the approach so that it could be subject to scientific evaluation. He wrote (p. 182): "We cannot begin to study the results of such a nebulous process as 'psychotherapy' in any meaningful way unless we can first state unambiguously what is done and for what reasons."

The Conversational Model is designed for treating patients whose problems arise from defects or disturbances in significant relationships. Hobson described how it "aims at the promotion of unlearning and of new learning in a dialogue between persons. A situation is created in which problems are disclosed, explored, understood, and modified within a therapeutic conversation" (p. 182). In essence, the therapist is trying to reach understanding of a patient, especially the patient's current feelings in therapy; to articulate, share, and modify such understanding through a "mutual feeling language"; and to promote insight and explore the meanings of the person's experience and conduct. Bob Hobson was especially concerned to foster the "development of the dynamic relationship of aloneness-togetherness" (p 183). He wrote:

> explanatory interpretations are not the goal of therapy, nor are they essential for "insight." They are useful in organizing, in making sense of, immediate experiences and helping the acknowledgement of disclaimed actions; but these formulations are

important only in so far as they promote on-going, understanding conversations in a language of feeling which is developing *now*. (p. 198)

A formal version of the approach became known as Psychodynamic Interpersonal Therapy, admirably summarized and discussed by Guthrie (1999).

Therapeutic approach

As in each of the examples of brief psychotherapy given here, the principles outlined should not be viewed as the be all and end all of treatment. In the case of the Conversational Model, for example, Bob Hobson stressed that the prime task of a psychotherapist is *"to go on learning more about how to listen"* (italics in the original, p. 208).

Psychotherapy needs to take place within an agreed timeframe, and the number of sessions and date of ending are made clear at the outset. Within this structure, the therapist embarks on the task of understanding the patient's emotional experience, through tentative exploration. The therapist tends:

- to focus on the here and now relation between patient and therapist, and be prepared to address hidden feelings that are either evident but unavailable to the patient, or missing when they would be appropriate to what is being recounted or relived

- to make statements (rather than asking questions) to express the therapist's understanding of a patient's experience

- to employ metaphors and other "living symbols" to capture and explore a patient's emotional states

- to employ first person words "I" and "we," the use of which "affirms the aim of a conversation between two separate and yet related responsible persons who, alone and together, claim their actions" (p. 196).

- in due course, to offer "understanding hypotheses" about reasons that might underlie the patient's difficulties

- to point out recurring themes in the patient's different relationships, both past and present, including links with the patient–therapist relationship; and to indicate connections with the patient's symptoms or other presenting complaints

- to aim at the "reduction of fear associated with separation, loss, and abandonment" (p. 196), and to draw attention to moments in psychotherapy when the patient does or feels something new.

The therapist needs to set interventions in a meaningful sequence, so that for instance, staying with feelings comes first and articulating explanatory hypotheses only later. Serious thought is given to the ending of treatment, both for its personal significance to the patient and because of the need to review the value and limitations of what has occurred in the course of psychotherapy.

Here is a brief sequence of edited dialogue (omitting most of the commentary that appears in the original text, as well as some of the verbal exchanges) between Bob Hobson and a patient Freda, distilled from Chapter 2 of *Forms of Feeling* (R.F. Hobson 1985, pp. 22–24: I adopt "RFH" and "Freda" from the original):

FREDA: It just seems to be bottled up. And I feel guilty over that, as though there's something wrong with me—that I should be crying and yet I just can't cry.

RFH: Well, I think you *are* feeling a lot *inside*.

[from text, p. 22: "As I say these words, I move toward her speaking with my hands. My fingers move back and forwards between my tummy and hers. I then point to the space between us."]

GAP

FREDA: There's ... this terrible empty feeling I've got inside.

RFH [from text p. 23: "I speak with my hands, gently moving them up and down with palms towards her."]: Sort of ... empty.

FREDA: Empty. Just empty.

RFH (discovering his right hand is over his heart): You put your hand about here.

FREDA (repeating RFH's movement): Just about here. Emptiness.

RFH: Mm.

FREDA: Just empty.

RFH: Just as if there is nothing there at all ... Let me make a guess ... er ... I think that there are times ... when you feel bad ... that you can't love people enough.

FREDA: That's just it.

Freda then elaborates on her lack of love for her husband and mother, and her guilt about this.

Overall, then, the Conversational Model encourages mutual exploration between patient and therapist. The tone is collaborative, and the primary aim is to achieve, express, and share interpersonal understanding, both verbally and nonverbally, especially in relation to what is happening in the present interaction between patient and therapist. It is this process that affords the patient new ways of seeing (insights) and provides the basis for change.

Brief Psychoanalytic Therapy (BPT)

Background and aims

In developing BPT, I have tried to refine how a rather specific developmentally grounded psychoanalytic therapeutic technique might be characterized and applied in the form of a brief therapy. The core developmental principle is that if a psychotherapist whom a patient implicates in his or her repeating patterns of relationship offers emotional understanding and containment, then often, but not always, changes in those patterns can be effected. Treatment provides an opportunity for a patient to acquire new capacities to tolerate and think about difficult states of mind through the patient's experience of the *psychotherapist's* capacity to encompass and think about the patient's patterns of relatedness in treatment. When a patient internalizes what he or she experiences interpersonally, in relation to the therapist, then this alters the patient's own potential for managing emotional difficulties.

Therapeutic approach

In BPT there is a relatively restricted focus upon the transference relationship between therapist and patient. The approach involves a *particular* way of working in the transference, with a special focus on moment-to-moment shifts in patient–therapist relatedness. It is *not* assumed that in a 16-session treatment, one needs to modify/amplify/complement transference-based interpretative work, providing one respects the altered temporal framework. Which is not to say that only interpretative work happens in BPT.

The first principle of technique is that the psychotherapist should be open to listen to the patient, in such a way as to register on an emotional level what is happening between the patient and therapist in the present encounter. The therapist's focus is upon the ways in which a patient relates to the psychotherapist him/herself—to discern how the patient presents him/herself as someone to be related to in particular ways, and to be sensitive to the patient's efforts to establish and maintain his or her own emotional balance in order to avoid certain interpersonal-cum-intrapsychic difficulties or conflicts. The second principle, which in a way is already embedded in the first, is that this focus on the transference should be informed by the therapist's analysis of the countertransference, that is, his or her own emotional responses to the patient's engagement.

Treatment strategies are not prescribed, but therapists can consult a manual that illustrates how the particular orientation of BPT is likely to be expressed in a therapist's interventions. In particular, interpretations tend to be anchored in the here and now, with a focus on how the patient experiences the therapist, and on what the patient is trying to *do* to maintain his/her equilibrium. The therapist mostly comments on what is happening in current emotional transactions, often on the basis of evidence that is available for explicit comment, rather than inviting the patient to reflect on conjectures. The approach does *not* entail a specific, mutually formulated focus to which one returns (after all, the transference is the focus), and there is no written summary to share with the patient at the conclusion of treatment.

Here is dialogue from a BPT transcript that we shall revisit in Chapter 6:

T (THERAPIST): I think that you do it here, too, you always talk … I was still speaking and you really formulated an answer. Just now as we have spoken, when I was saying that it is difficult for you to stay with the things that you don't know, in the hope of connecting with you and helping you to stay with that, you then say, you then come back with a counter-argument and it is a way of getting away from that confusion, not-knowing, panic.

PT (PATIENT): I agree and I'm not gonna counter-attack or argue. The thing is I feel that I would have too much to lose to just be, to just go with the flow and just show my feelings. The shell that I have is probably very, very thick and it just …

T: You see it's not as if you don't, you're not in touch with feelings or you don't know these feelings, because you tell me about them, but then you move away from it. For example, you tell me there's confusion, you tell me that there are these feelings that you don't like and you don't want to approach them in your mind, you move away from them. You say that the sessions are ending and that there are feelings about that; what then happens is that we don't go deeper, you can't explore them further. You quickly move away to what you know …

Here the therapist and patient are (mostly) strongly engaged in eyeball-to-eyeball give-and-take, as the therapist registers and tracks current interpersonal engagement and the states of mind such engagement seems to involve and to avoid.

Commonalities

Now one might say (and many a clinician might believe) that each of these treatments are very similar in that they are relationship-orientated talking therapies. It is not uncommon for critics of dynamic psychotherapy to comment wryly on psychotherapists' heated disagreements over trivial distinctions. There is a view that all talking psychotherapies are much of a muchness.

Indeed, there are important commonalities among the approaches I have described. In each, a therapist and patient meet together face to face and engage in a communicative process that has an explicit structure, for instance in relation to the timing of sessions and length of treatment. In each, the therapist pays serious attention to the patient's presenting complaints and to wider aspects of the patient's experience, especially in their social relations. Each form of psychotherapy is intended to help the patient reflect upon his or her experiences from new perspectives. In the course of therapy, it is expected that the process may tap potentially relevant feelings of which the patient has been unaware. As explicitly stated by advocates of several of the approaches, it is perfectly appropriate to begin with the "surface" of what transpires between patient and therapist—something to which all the therapies are alert—and by this route, to gain access to depths of a person's emotional life.

These points of similarity are far from trivial. For many a patient, the experience of meeting a professional who devotes care and attention not just to the person's illness, but more especially to his or her subjective experiences and struggles can be profoundly moving and significant. Beyond this, one needs to bear in mind the risk of oversimplifying and even distorting matters when any given psychotherapy is practiced in a variety of ways, some of which blur seemingly clear boundaries among techniques.

On the other hand, one could take the view that the therapies described fall into groupings that are as different as (say) anxiolytic, antidepressant, and mild antipsychotic medications. They might be indicated for quite different conditions and/or patients, or perhaps appropriately delivered by different kinds of psychotherapist. The developmental principles underlying each psychotherapeutic enterprise overlap *and* diverge, and in certain respects seem to be as distinctive as the pharmacological principles underlying the effects of different psychotropic drugs. Here I focus on a single set of contrasts.

The therapeutic stance

At the heart of psychotherapy is the therapist's stance. Among some psychotherapists, it is taken for granted that the therapist should make efforts to establish a friendly but formal supportive and collaborative relationship. To be sure, an underlying therapeutic alliance is critical for the cooperative work that every kind of dynamic psychotherapy entails. Yet there do seem to be substantial and significant differences in *how* therapists conceive that alliance should be strengthened, and how it operates. Not only the joint focus, but also how patient and therapist jointly work on that focus, are in contention.

The initial phases of treatment illustrate divergences among psychotherapies especially clearly. If the IPT therapist works to instil hope and an expectation of change, or the CAT therapist gives homework to further the task of mapping out precipitants and sequelae to symptoms, or the DIT therapist assists the patient to think in terms of thoughts and feelings, explores new ways of dealing with problems and encourages reflection, or the ISTDP therapist makes it abundantly clear he or she is on the patient's side in the battle against untoward defences, or the therapist using the Conversational Model conveys openness and flexibility when embarking on a tentative mutual dialogue, how could these kinds of patient-centered intervention be faulted? Surely the BPT therapist, earnestly intent to address and foster the unfolding of patient–therapist engagement, runs the risk that he or she will fail to cement an effective therapeutic collaboration, neglect the value of detailed history taking, deflect from truly mutual engagement, and even undermine the personal authority and dignity of the patient.

But consider this. In commencing on psychotherapy in a particular way, a therapist is conveying a lot about his or her orientation to the patient's difficulties, and to the respective roles that patient and therapist are expected to adopt in the treatment that ensues. Very often, patients are highly tuned to what a given therapist seems to be wishing to achieve, and soon discern what the therapist will receive with either approval or disapproval. Patients may respond to their perception of the therapist's wishes or needs in various ways, of course: for instance, by enthusiastically pitching in, or by trying to please or placate the therapist, or by subtly undermining or passively resisting the therapist's efforts.

Therefore the question arises: in balance, is it best to assert or strongly imply the importance of a particular kind of therapeutic alliance between patient and therapist, and then press on unless or until obstructions to the treatment become apparent, or is it best to explore what the patient's attitudes, expectations and reactions are now, even from the beginning of treatment? Do assertive therapeutic strategies drive important emotional issues underground when these are in urgent need of attention, or do they recruit a patient's motivation for the task in hand, and merely postpone the emergence of significant repeating patterns of relatedness?

Most of the psychotherapeutic approaches I have listed in this chapter espouse a hefty dose of interrogation and instruction, especially at the beginning of treatment. In contrast, a therapist in the style of the Conversational Model or BPT proceeds in a way designed to reveal, slowly but persistently, how a patient experiences the therapist's stance and communication. In BPT in particular, the focus is on how a patient's expectations and active shaping of engagement with the therapist constrain, amplify, disclose, or disguise what is really happening in the therapeutic relationship.

It is not that the BPT therapist is under instruction to avoid asking questions about symptomatology or the patient's history. However, if the transference is likely to be obscured by direct enquiries, it makes sense to delay more detailed questioning, insofar as this is indicated, until a point at which questions might clarify the patterns of relationship that are emerging, and have a lesser impact in molding therapist–patient exchanges. Nor is the therapist disguising his or her own therapeutic attitude. It soon becomes manifest that the therapist is trying to understand the truth of what is happening in the session, on the patient's behalf.

Contrasts in therapeutic orientation crystallize in the matter of arriving at a shared formulation. This figures prominently in the early part of treatment of many of the approaches considered above, and casts its spotlight or shadow, depending on one's viewpoint, on what follows. The dominant view is that an agreed formulation is a valuable distillation, whether of the problems (at the beginning of treatment) or insights gained (at the end), a reminder of what needs to be in focus (at the beginning), and a bulwark against the vagaries of memory and the passing of time (at the end).

A BPT therapist is inclined to think that the "formulation" approach is oversimplifying and premature (and incidentally, although a feature of PIT, I think I recall my father expressing mixed feelings about formulations, and I do not see it as a cardinal feature of the Conversational Model). More importantly, and even at the end of treatment, the *process* of jointly formulating may have untoward consequences. Formulation building establishes an intellectual frame in which patient and therapist have this objective something—the formulation—to *talk about*. Even if this avoids the danger of leaving the patient "pinned and wriggling on the wall" (Eliot, 1969, p. 14, originally 1917), a narrative "it" has been created as a focus of joint attention. This topic of mutual interest may allow for, perhaps even encourage, a patient to speak of him or herself from a distanced vantage point, at one remove from his or her immediate experience—and specifically, at a remove from his or her immediate experience in relation to the therapist. There are costs attached if a patient is recruited into the role of co-therapist.

Meanwhile, we do not have to assume that a brief intervention either does or does not need an explicitly formulated focus. Attention to *that* kind of focus is just one way to keep a therapy on track. A focus on the here-and-now transference can do so, too. Very often, a relatively small number of issues repeatedly re-emerge in different ways in the transference, and a therapist may be dogged in highlighting recurrent themes. Arguably, what is happening in the transference is that which is most emotionally available and alive, *and* that which affords the most penetrating focus for what needs to be addressed to promote change. So, too, we really do not know about the beneficial or constricting implications for a patient's self-experience and emotional perspective, when he or she carries away a written formulation at the end of treatment.

I want to return to the matter of respect for patients. Does BPT represent the return of the arrogant, dogmatic, and impervious stance of the all-knowing, though perhaps mythical, analytic therapist? Well, few would disagree that it is respectful for any therapist to point out what is happening in the patient–therapist relation, when there is evidence for the happenings in question. It is a hallmark of BPT that there is usually a close temporal as well as meaningful relation between a therapist's comments and the evidence for those comments in the patient–therapist interaction. If it is necessary or helpful, the BPT therapist can point to the basis on which observations are made. Whether the patient accepts or rejects the intervention, the therapist is committed to reviewing and perhaps revising what he or she had thought and said. Note that respect here works on several levels at once: there is respect for the patient's current mode of relatedness, respect for the truth of what is actually taking place at any given moment in the therapeutic relationship, and respect for the patient's potential to apprehend, explore, and ultimately commit to what emerges as true. Of course it is possible to construe this as the imposition of a therapist's version of what is true, and readers will need to judge from the detailed case material that is offered in subsequent chapters of the book, whether this concern is justified.

Let me be blunt. I confess that as a patient, I would find it uncomfortable for a therapist to suggest we "work together" on my problems in the ways proposed by some forms of psychotherapy. I would feel both restricted by and resentful about the presumption that we could or should arrive at an explicit formulation of my difficulties. I would question how far seeming egalitarianism was disguising subtle condescension; I would be uneasy that the vital complementarity in our positions—therapist as therapist, myself as patient—was being denied; and I would wonder what had happened to convert "myself" into a topic that could be condensed into a brief narrative. Toward the conclusion of treatment, I would prefer to work on the meaning of the ending, shake hands, and leave to assume my own life. I would be glad to take with me whatever of the therapy and therapist I found valuable, and not have to pocket a formulation. I am told other patients feel differently, something I need to acknowledge and understand.

Overall, the critical question is this: What *kind* of stance is optimal for identifying and/or addressing the truth of a patient's emotional difficulties? *If* the task of identifying here-and-now instances of the person's problematic and often highly conflictual relatedness patterns and defences in the transference is so important—and by no means all the therapeutic approaches I have outlined deem this so central a matter—then how is one to proceed? *If* a principal goal is to achieve depth, coherence, and directness of interpersonal contact between therapist and patient—a goal that the Conversational Model and BPT consider critical for the *kind* of insight that brings profound change—then what are the most appropriate means to accomplish this?

Now I shall say just a little about the evidence that short-term psychodynamic treatments can be effective.

Effectiveness

I propose to deal swiftly with the question of evidence for effectiveness of short-term psychodynamic psychotherapy. One reason is that, given the heterogeneity among treatments and therapists involved in the studies, it is not clear how much bearing the results might have on the question of whether BPT is effective. Nevertheless, it is worth making a single point, rather firmly, for the reason that critics (often rivals) of psychodynamic forms of psychotherapy disseminate the view that there is little evidence in favor of such approaches. Meta-analyses of relevant research, including randomized controlled trials, suggest otherwise (e.g., Abbass et al. 2014; Leichsenring, Rabung, and Leibing 2004; Leichsenring 2005; Gerber et al. 2011).

For the present purposes, it may be helpful to provide just two examples of specific studies. The first concerns Psychodynamic Interpersonal Therapy, which as I have described, derives from the Conversational Model of R.F. Hobson. The study was conducted by Guthrie and her colleagues (1999), and concerned high utilizers of psychiatric services and, more specifically, patients with neurotic conditions who did not respond to psychiatric treatment. This was a randomized controlled trial of Psychodynamic Interpersonal Therapy plus treatment as usual, in relation to treatment as usual alone. The treatment was manualized, and adherence to the approach was evaluated. Patients were assessed on entry, at end of the eight-week trial, and at follow-up six months later. The findings were that improvements at six-month follow-up were greater for psychodynamic psychotherapy than treatment as usual in measures of psychological distress and social functioning. Although there had been similar service utilization during treatment, over the six-month follow-up, patients who had received psychodynamic psychotherapy had fewer days as in-patients and fewer GP consultations and contacts with the practice nurse, received less medication and less informal care from relatives. The extra cost of treatment was recouped within six months through reductions in health care use.

The second example is a study by Milrod et al. (2007), and was a randomized controlled trial of psychoanalytic psychotherapy compared with relaxation training for panic disorder among patients, some of whom were also depressed. Treatments were given twice weekly for 12 weeks. Patients in psychodynamic treatment had significantly more reduction of panic symptoms, and greater improvement in psychosocial functioning.

The upshot of these and other studies summarized in the meta-analyses cited above is that there *is* evidence for the potential benefit of brief psychodynamic therapies for a range of patients. As I have said, this does not mean that BPT is effective, or rather, that it is effective for certain patients, as delivered by skilled therapists. In style and brief format, however, BPT seems broadly in line with other approaches for which there is formal evidence of value. Whether it may be more or less effective, or (as I would prefer to think of this) of greater or lesser value in promoting certain kinds of developmental, clinically relevant change, is simply not known.

It is time to offer a more vivid portrayal of Brief Psychoanalytic Therapy, through extended clinical vignettes.

Chapter 3

A first case history

Introduction

In this and the following chapter, I introduce the practice of Brief Psychoanalytic Therapy through two clinical vignettes. Here my aim is to provide an overview of what goes on in treatment, rather than to focus upon specific therapeutic interventions that the treatment entails. A down-to-earth description of two patients' course of psychotherapy should help readers to grasp what it means for a therapist to work in the transference, and to see how this can enable patients to change. Subsequently, in Chapter 5, I dwell on verbatim excerpts from a session with a third patient in order to track moment-by-moment patient–therapist transactions. Following this, in Chapter 6, I take stock and recapitulate the principles of Brief Psychoanalytic Therapy by laying out the Treatment Manual. This will provide a springboard for fresh takes on the nature of the approach, in the second half of the book.

In each of the clinical accounts, I have altered significant parts of the descriptions of individual patients, in order to maintain confidentiality. Each patient gave written permission for disguised clinical material to be published. The alterations I have made are intended to obscure the identities of the people involved, but do not affect the accounts of their therapeutic engagement.

The woman described in the present chapter was seen in an out-patient clinic for approximately 16 sessions of once-weekly treatment. I had conducted the initial two assessment interviews, and subsequently became the person's psychotherapist. Here I shall describe my initial consultations as well as the subsequent psychotherapy, because each was conducted according to similar principles. Not only this, but the first consultation involved far more than "assessing," and constituted the beginning of treatment.

In order to prepare the reader for clinical descriptions that might otherwise seem unsettling or perplexing, it might help to anticipate certain features of the therapeutic transactions to be described.

Firstly, I should offer comment on the way I conduct initial assessment consultations. I have discussed and illustrated my approach to such interviews in a book I edited, entitled *Consultations in Psychoanalytic Psychotherapy* (Hobson 2013). Perhaps most unnerving to many psychotherapists and clients alike, I begin the interviews in a relatively unstructured way, introducing myself formally ("My name is Dr. Hobson") and saying how long has been set aside for the meeting, but otherwise declining to explain what the patient is expected to do or say. This does *not* mean I subject the patient to lengthy unproductive silences or expose the patient to disturbance or trauma beyond the minimum necessary to allow each patient's anxieties and ways of coping with those anxieties to become available for joint work. I trust the vignettes that follow will convey how I have the patient's interests at heart. My aim is to gain access to, and help the patient deal with, emotional issues that really matter if we are to address the patient's presenting problems.

Secondly, descriptions of the initial encounters as well as the psychotherapy that follows should convey what it means to engage in a certain kind of "working in the transference." This particular approach entails a focus on the minutiae of patient–therapist transactions. I pay special attention to patients' efforts to maintain their equilibrium by exercising control over the nature of their interpersonal engagement with myself as therapist. The rationale is that almost always, this approach holds the key for revealing and addressing patients' difficulties, for tackling how anxieties and defensive maneuvers give shape to their emotional life, and for tapping into their strengths and potential commitment to psychoanalytic psychotherapy.

Finally by way of introduction, I would like to return to the issue of personal development. I hope it will become apparent that over the course of psychotherapy, even over the course of an initial consultation, there is the prospect for development and change in a patient's relationship with the therapist. I am always hopeful that by the end of the first consultation, and whatever unpleasantness might have been experienced at the outset, something like the beginnings of mutual understanding will have been achieved—or at least, the possibility of such understanding will have been registered—between patient and therapist. Often these meetings are deeply moving.

Case vignette

Ms A was a single woman in her late thirties who had been referred for chronic fatigue and came with a variety of medical diagnoses. Throughout her early life as an only child, both she and her parents had been afflicted with physical disorders. She had received various treatments, and now expressed a wish to be more productive and develop a social life. In a questionnaire, she described herself as "physically, mentally and emotionally exhausted."

The initial consultation

The opening phase of the consultation

Ms A arrived on time for her assessment consultation. She had a downtrodden look, and tousled fair hair. She asked me where she should start. When I looked at her but did not reply, she said how if there is no structure in a situation and she does not get feedback, she does not know where to begin. She said that once before she had had a therapist who sat in silence, and it was not very helpful. Perhaps she herself could sit here saying nothing, or she might just talk about things that are not important.

I took up with Ms A how she seemed to trust neither herself nor myself. She might not deal with the most important matters, and I might simply sit in silence, which would be useless. At the same time, I added, she referred to a possible option of becoming silent herself.

Ms A said that she was simply not used to this kind of situation, so unstructured. I said she conveyed a need to have someone either taking the lead, or reacting to what she said. Although her initial stance was to half-dismiss this notion, she soon returned to say how difficult it is if she doesn't get a response.

Ms A's emotional state at this time was not persecuted. I had the feeling that although she was uncomfortable, still she was well in control both of herself and myself. She took off her jacket, conveying how she was not going to walk out. She made it clear she felt my stance was unhelpful, and contrasted this with a different form of therapy she had received some while ago, where there was something to focus upon, and the therapist was able to reveal things to her. However, her therapist had to leave with some changes in her professional circumstances. Although initially Ms A did not comment on the significance of this, it was clear that it was important for her that the treatment had ended prematurely.

Reflections on the opening phase My purpose here is not to dwell on the special circumstances surrounding an initial consultation, but to point out certain features of what transpired in this first meeting that pertain to the conduct of Brief Psychoanalytic Therapy. In some ways, these features are all the more striking when they occur at the very beginning of therapeutic contact with a patient.

Firstly, I allowed the initial moments of the session to unfold before I said anything. The point was not to provoke the patient, but to see whether, in this inevitably stressful (and uniquely revealing) part of our engagement, it would be possible to discern anxieties that were specific to Ms A. Just as importantly, I sought indication of how Ms A dealt with those anxieties, and how she related to myself as a therapist who was responsible for what was happening. In pursuing this approach, I was aware that it would be challenging and stressful for us both.

Perhaps it goes without saying that in circumstances such as these, I would not allow a patient's anxiety to rise beyond a certain level. But if one tries too hard or too quickly to circumvent anxiety, not to mention hostility towards oneself as a therapist, then important aspects of a person's character and emotional state are likely to remain undisclosed. In holding back from doing what would have been most comfortable for Ms A *and* myself, namely to tell her what I expected and to begin to shape the session, perhaps by asking questions, I led us to experience something less scripted and emotionally edgy than would otherwise have been the case.

In the event, what emerged in Ms A was a subtle blend of anxiety, anger, and hurt. Ms A was willing and able to express her feelings to myself in an impressively direct manner. Her anxieties were real but not unmanageable, and already I had gained a sense of her potential forthrightness. Although she insisted that she needed to be guided, it seemed she was more resourceful than she claimed.

Of my own interventions, I would simply note how I tried to say things about emotionally charged issues in the patient's attitude to me and what was taking place between us, for which there was good evidence in what Ms A had said. If the contents of my remarks seem almost self-evident, they were far from trivial. They touched on Ms A's trust and mistrust, not just in relation to myself but also to herself and the productivity of our meeting. In addition, I conveyed that I had registered her own potential for retaliation, in that she might go silent in response to my silence (which in fact, was brief). My statements captured what Ms A communicated to me, and had a direct bearing on our emotional interchange in the session. Of course, in making comments about Ms A and her experience (or potential experience) of me, I revealed a lot about my stance and orientation toward Ms A. Even in these first few minutes of our meeting, Ms A had learnt much about me and the way I was trying understand her—and what I was prepared to risk, including confrontation and unpleasantness, in the pursuit of such understanding.

The second phase of the consultation

What happened next was that Ms A began to soften and become more emotional. She looked to me, asking if I had any handkerchiefs. She saw there were no tissues on the low table next to her (this happened to be unusual, but Ms A could not have known that), and then reached into her bag for a tissue of her own.

Clearly Ms A was deeply affected by my failure to have tissues to offer her. I remarked on this. She explained that any psychotherapist would have handkerchiefs available, it is one of the things that psychotherapists do to provide a setting. She conveyed strongly—and I articulated this—how could I be trusted, if I could not even provide tissues? This was an idea that came to prey upon her mind for much of the remainder of the session, threatening to undermine her chance to discover whether or not I could understand her or take her seriously. When I commented on this, she acknowledged it was true. She drew a parallel with the way her previous therapy had ended: what really affected her, was that the therapist could not advise her on where else she might go. It was as if her individual needs were not considered.

Ms A said there was perhaps more difficulty with me being a man. She described how her father is a closed-off person, and other male relatives had been insensitive towards her. Her mother, on the other hand, was much more available and caring about her concerns. So she feels that she has put herself forward to the males in her family, but got very little back.

By this time, two other things had become apparent. Firstly, as I commented, there seemed to be a pressure of feeling within Ms A. Either she kept her feelings under tight rein, or they threatened to come out in an uncontrollable way. She referred to how this is only a short meeting, and she might go out soggy and all over the place, and she doesn't want that.

Secondly, I recognized a certain restriction in my own experience in relation to Ms A. Although I was given some access to her having emotional difficulties, at least in the sense of witnessing her struggles, at the same time I felt there was little scope to communicate personal understanding of her situation, in such a way that both she and I might feel relief. She maintained control over what was allowed to happen between us, even when she had become more emotional.

At several points I was able to address this limitation in interpersonal engagement. For instance, she would look at me briefly, but then look away before I could give any clear reaction. Even when I said things that seemed to be understanding, and that apparently she registered, she did not appear to be satisfied herself, nor did she give me the feeling that what I was offering was satisfying. When I remarked on this, Ms A acknowledged that indeed, this was happening. More than this, she felt it was important.

At around this point in the consultation, Ms A said that on the questionnaire, one of the things she had written was that she gets very tired, and she is feeling that now. I said no wonder, when she invests so much energy in keeping control both over herself, and over me in our exchanges. Again she registered this, and returned to it later, saying it was true.

Reflections on the second phase The tissue incident was important on a number of levels. Firstly, Ms A asked for something she needed, and could reasonably expect. When I failed to provide tissues, it turned out she could supply some for herself. I wondered whether this was another pointer to her partly hidden resourcefulness. More important, however, was the way it revealed Ms A's potential to become preoccupied with seeming evidence that I was not to be trusted to anticipate and provide for her needs, especially as these related to her vulnerability. More important still, when I took up this issue she acknowledged how it was true that such a matter could prey on her mind. But she was also explicit to me about how strongly she can feel her individual needs are not taken into consideration.

It was possible to explore other important aspects of Ms A's current mental state, including her wish to keep herself under control. It felt that she and I were able to work together in building up a picture of some of the anxieties she was facing, and her means to keep her particular mode of equilibrium.

Meanwhile, my feelings in the countertransference—that is, the way I was coming to experience the engagement with Ms A for myself, in response to the ways she was relating to my own behavior and thinking—were becoming more coherent. From very early on I had felt pressure from Ms A to provide her with (as she more or less explicitly expressed it) what any patient would be justified in expecting, including guidance and sympathetic responsiveness. As the session progressed, I became more convinced that Ms A was reluctant to allow me to connect with her in a way that could satisfy either of us. I was able to point out specific moments when this happened in the course of our verbal interchanges. On the other hand, Ms A could grasp what I was showing her, and see that it held significance—*and* was willing and able to say as much to me. These were no small matters, and spoke volumes about Ms A's quickness of mind. Most importantly, our serious work in addressing Ms A's evasion of personal, committed engagement led us to a new kind of contact, in which there were moments of emotionally convincing mutual acknowledgment. This, too, was testament to Ms A's potential, not least in relation to her capacity to use a therapist's input productively.

Finally, there was the short but intriguing episode of Ms A saying how she gets very tired. She introduced this as being a kind of trait that she has, and against that background, how it has come on her now. I think her saying this at this particular point in the session was a kind of bid. Partly it was an appeal, but also in part a maneuver to induce me to be indulgent and allow her respite from the work we were doing. My response was to re-frame the episode in relation to the specifics of what she was doing here and now, with me.

The final phase of the consultation

I asked Ms A whether she dreams. She paused, and then said that one dream was of her standing on some blue girders at the top of a skyscraper, and she looked up and it was as if she was deep under water, and scuba divers were swimming near the surface. She went straight on to another dream, one she had had last night, in which again she was by herself, and there were some purses laid out and she was desperate to get some change, but didn't want to be thought to be stealing. She reached for one of the purses, but then withdrew. She offered some reflections about wanting to buy a new purse but sending one back, and then paused.

I said she didn't say whether or not she was interested in any thoughts I might have about the meaning of these dreams. She said well, she did pause after recounting the dreams, and she thought that was a kind of invitation. I pointed out how she does not open herself to asking, when she might be turned down.

I said that, at least, both dreams showed her by herself. Although the scuba divers could descend to meet her, in fact both dreams give a sense of a life not fully lived. Once again she looked thoughtful. I took up how here she seemed to find what I said meaningful, and yet neither of us could really feel the satisfaction of that. She agreed, and said yes, they are meaningful. Once again, she moved away quickly so we could not register together the dreams' significance, nor develop shared understanding—and yet again, when I took this up, she could see what I meant.

I asked Ms A what she felt she needed. She was explicit that she had found this meeting helpful, particularly my picking up how she does not stay with moments of connection. She had thought she wanted cognitive-behavioral treatment, but now she feels that this is what she wishes to pursue. I expressed my view that, for her specifically, cognitive-behavioral treatment might play into her ways of keeping things at a certain level. Ms A nodded.

At first, Ms A agreed to join the waiting list for group psychotherapy. Subsequently, however, her family doctor wrote to me to ask if I might see her again, describing how Ms A had felt unable to commit herself to group psychotherapy and would prefer to see someone individually.

Reflections on the final phase Often, about two-thirds of the way through an assessment consultation, I ask a patient whether he or she can tell me a dream. In Ms A's case, I am sure there was much, much more meaning in her dreams than I felt able to pursue. The two most striking issues, namely the spaces over which the figures were distributed in the first dream, and in the second dream, the facts that she was desperate "to get some change," didn't want to be thought stealing, and reached for a purse but then withdrew, almost certainly reflected something profound. They presented an intriguing picture of aspects of Ms A's current interaction with myself. However, I chose to focus on the process of my connecting (or not) with Ms A over the meanings, for the reason that I considered this the most pressing matter for the future of her psychotherapy. My view of what was most important seemed to correspond with that of Ms A, because when subsequently I asked her what she felt she needed, she made specific reference to my picking up how she does not stay with moments of connection.

Follow-up consultation

On the occasion of our second meeting, Ms A gave a big sigh as she came out of the lift, and a further big sigh as she sat down. This initial part of our meeting was spent with her pressing her case—and with little sign of expecting to be listened to or believed—that with her various problems, she really couldn't be sure she could commit to coming and spending an hour and a half at a group over such a long period. Indeed, she has asked to cut down sessions in a supportive treatment she's receiving already. She just can't focus for long enough. Besides, even today she has a migraine. At this point she asked me to further lower the blinds. She continued that she is about to be seen for other complaints she has.

I stressed how again and again, her experiences with doctors (to which she had made specific reference) were unsatisfactory and unsatisfying. No-one really seemed to know what was happening and how to help her. She felt there was so much to say, I continued, and it was difficult to get it across. She felt unheard, not taken seriously, frustrated, unsatisfied, and on top of all that, she is expected to do things that are simply not possible.

Slowly she began to reflect on what I had been saying, and in particular, to consider whether we were seeing something of her habitual way of experiencing others.

I agreed with Ms A that she could not commit to something, if she simply could not commit herself. I said I still felt that group psychotherapy was the treatment of choice, but it is no good trying something impossible. At the same time, I said there is a problem. Whatever her physical problems, there is a side to Ms A that takes things a certain way, as here when she almost never registers when I am highlighting positive aspects of herself. I said that as a matter of fact, I can offer to see her myself for a brief psychotherapy. Momentarily (as in her reported dream) she withdrew from my offer and reverted to saying she would try a group if she could. Then rather suddenly she said she would come to see me.

The course of psychotherapy

Despite encouraging aspects of the first meeting, I was not optimistic about psychotherapy with Ms A. Against the backdrop of longstanding physical complaints, Ms A's ailing stance seemed to have become entrenched as a *modus vivendi.* The follow-up consultation indicated how one should expect relapses to the *status quo,* and how one would need to tackle deeply felt resentments and frustrations.

The early part of treatment

I was somewhat taken aback, therefore, when, even over the first two sessions, it proved possible to make quite a lot of headway. Critical to progress were qualities in Ms A that had emerged at the initial assessment consultation. From that time and then throughout treatment, and especially when challenged, Ms A had the capacity to reflect on what she was doing in a way that was *not* so helpless nor fatalistic. Just as surprising and impressive, she could be generous in acknowledging my contribution to what was happening. For example, as she had stood up from her chair at the end of the second session, Ms A remarked: "I know it's short, but I feel a lot has happened in these two sessions, and I feel there is a chance of getting somewhere."

In the early sessions, the principal focus of the work was Ms A's characteristic way of protecting herself and nullifying the impact that anyone else might have on herself. I have already described how it was possible to address such maneuvers in the assessment consultation, and it was not difficult to point out how, especially when she felt she was in danger of not being taken seriously, she would institute now-familiar protective strategies. It was not merely that one could feel the abrupt shift in contact with Ms A as she lapsed into complaints or recriminations, but also that she herself began to see what I meant when I commented on her choosing to take this path. She could also appreciate how there was something profoundly important in this. She said she knows she presents herself as having these disorders, because it would be mean of anyone to question her reasons for being the way she is. I said she paralyzes people, in the nicest possible way.

Alongside this, of course, there was the task of examining anxieties and other difficult feelings Ms A was needing to avoid. In particular, we returned again and again to how sensitive she was to the way I treated her. Ms A could articulate this herself, and could see that this fact was deeply relevant for how she has felt for a long time. She described how she can easily feel that others do not appreciate all she does and has to put up with, or that others are trying to "put her into a box" in which they expect her to conform to norms, for instance over the time she is expected to get up from bed. How she resents that! Gradually she came to say how she knows she finds it very difficult to be open to other people. She can feel like she has been skinned, and her nerves raw.

I said how she and I do need to be aware just how hard it is for her to be open. She needs someone to be firm with her, if she is to face things.

It was possible to explore some sources of Ms A's feelings in her upbringing. In addition, it became more explicit how she could fashion her personal relations so that others had to endure *her* insensitivity and tendency to prejudice. I took up with her a very characteristic pattern in our exchanges, when she would begin with a "but …" and then talk as if to someone who is uncomprehending and deserving a fight. Invariably, she would end up frustrated and not fully in contact. This meant that *she* became unreceptive and unavailable, and in this way similar to relatives whom she had described as insensitive to herself.

The complication here was that often, I felt that Ms A's very insights into herself, or what she presented as her attempt to think through the causes of the way she is, were not enlisted in the service of change, but rather, to maintain the *status quo*. Even when she described parts of herself quite accurately, it was not yet with a view to challenging her own habits and battling to be different. She would often spend time talking about her illnesses at some length, to plant her flag. Or she would keep wiping her nose like a child, or speak of how she remains like a young bird in the nest. Such diversions would sap energy from more productive lines of exploration. She would remain untroubled by half-acknowledged, and potentially painful because unfulfilled, wishes and desires for herself and her own future.

In addition, there was a fine line between my acknowledging Ms A's struggles with her physical state, and being indulgent towards her. She felt she had to insist on describing her symptoms to a seemingly dismissive doctor, and it seemed that only intermittently could she recognize what she was doing. As her ambivalence over a variety of issues became more apparent, she was prone to switch to and fro among alternative stances in relation to herself as well as myself.

There were two times early in the treatment, when I had had to postpone sessions at short notice. Ms A told me, with striking directness, how she had felt and thought a lot about this. What is going on in his mind? What else might have come up that relegates her to second place? After all, she has made such an effort. Could it be I don't want to see her? She was hurt, but also angry, and it was impressive that instead of mulling this over in a hurt, hard-done-by way, Ms A was direct in her criticisms and her mixed feelings. I took up the forthrightness with which she communicated all this, and said how her feelings are justified— and I apologized. I also took up how she was being direct, apparently expecting me to listen and hear her, and neither retaliate nor collapse. She nodded.

I shall skip over the middle of treatment, much of which was spent addressing the themes already outlined, which reappeared again and again in the exchanges between Ms A and myself—although increasingly, in an atmosphere of trust and a shared understanding that allowed much greater flexibility of contact. Now I shall summarize the last two sessions.

The final sessions

Ms A arrived on time for the penultimate session. However, it took me three minutes to get through to reception to invite her to take the lift up to my floor. When she arrived in the lift—always a telling moment—Ms A gave an impression of freshness.

Once in the consulting room, Ms A said I will notice she is wearing a new top—not exactly colored, but not the kind of thing she would usually wear (and in fact, she was also wearing earrings which I had not noticed before, and bright nail varnish). I said yes, I do notice, and also want to say (here Ms A looked slightly concerned) that it took me three minutes to get through to reception, so we can add three minutes to her session if she can stay for the longer time. She said yes.

Ms A returned to say how she has been looking out for colored clothes to look nice. At winter time it's a problem, she has to wear high collars because otherwise she will catch a cold, other people can wear V-necks, she wears fleeces which she doesn't mind for the material but doesn't like the style; it's difficult, but perhaps she will at least look out for things to buy. I said it's notable how actually it's summer, when even she might wear a less high collar, but she immediately moves to talk about when it's colder and more difficult for her to find clothes. It's safer territory. She smiled in recognition, and continued that at least she's on the look out for things that might work for her, for possibilities.

In fact, she said, with this being the last but one session, she's been wondering how she might continue on with the kind of thing we have been discussing. She bought a book on Tai Chi, and one of the themes is being open to being open. She talked at some length about this. I said I think that one of the important things is that she needs me to appreciate she is pursuing such aims, not least so that in the future she will know that I am aware of what she is doing.

She said how these are the kinds of things she could not have done three months ago. She has moved a long way coming here. I said that one of the striking things is how on the one hand this is true, yet on the other it has not been that hard for her to come to trust me. And this is despite the hiccoughs we had over the choppy session times. I linked this with her taking over her family's financial management, and how what might have proved a really big hurdle for her turned out to be something that was difficult, yes, but not so very difficult. So, too, she finds she does not need to be a child and can be an adult, open to relationships, even though this carries risks.

Ms A said how it surprised her over the changed session times that she had not needed to punish me. She said that yes, she had felt angry and upset, but she forgave me. She also talked of how the most important thing coming here was that I was firm but fair, and didn't completely tell her she was wrong, she had to do it this other way—as she might tell herself. I said yes. I also said that in what she says, she indicates she could value how I wouldn't let her get away with things. At such times, she did not necessarily experience me as criticizing her. I said I thought she had come with feelings of resentment, but to her surprise found these were not so powerful. And in the case of the problems with sessions, she did express her negative feelings and actually felt I took them seriously. She said yes, definitely.

I said that, of course, this also presents her with a problem. She looked at me quizzically. I said that if it's not such a big thing that she can do things she felt she couldn't, then a whole world of possibilities opens up. If she can trust enough to have courage to wear different clothes and even be a bit sexy, then she can't go back and think these things are just not for her. She said she thinks she may be giving up her perfectionism, allowing things to be less controlled. Here the session ended.

The final session was very moving. She came out of the lift wearing a pink/purple top and smart jeans, and had had her hair cut attractively.

She talked of shifts in her vision of her parents, and how fragile and potentially explosive she feels her parents' relationship and the home situation to be. She had been trying to persuade her mother to see a psychologist to allow herself more space, but her mother does not feel able to be defiant or obstinate or whatever it takes to make a life of her own.

At several points, Ms A was tearful about what the loss of the sessions, and what the relationship with myself, meant to her. She thought she was probably very angry about the brevity of the treatment, but sadness was her strongest feeling. I took up how I thought she was protecting me somewhat, by being sensible. Ms A nodded. She felt it was so important that she had felt heard without needing to batter away, and that I had witnessed her change. She said it's not just talking about how things can be different, but actually experiencing them. As Ms A stood up to leave, and in tears, she said: "It's been fantastic, a dramatic voyage."

In a client satisfaction questionnaire completed at the end of treatment, Ms A wrote of improvements in a range of her difficulties (a matter also reflected in scores on standardized self-report questionnaires), and described how she herself was better at dealing with problems. "I think differently now about the problems—they don't seem quite so big." She wrote that she felt she had been treated with a lot of respect, and felt "very satisfied" with the way her treatment was managed. "I got off to a shaky start for various reasons but in a funny way even that in the end was helpful."

The nature of Brief Psychoanalytic Therapy

What might this case history contribute to an emerging picture of Brief Psychoanalytic Treatment?

Certain things stand out. First and foremost, important matters can be addressed, and development promoted, in the course of a 16-session treatment. Ms A illustrates how one factor in such development is whether the person's strengths can be recruited in the struggle to change—strengths that may emerge over shorter as well as longer periods of psychotherapy.

Of course, one might raise doubts about the genuineness or depth of the changes that *seemed* to have taken place in Ms A over the course of treatment. Perhaps the benefits might have come from support or suggestion. Even if the gains were substantial and not illusory, they might have derived from factors that had little to do with the specifics of the interventions.

I have a three-part response to such skepticism, each of which concerns evidence. Firstly, I would acknowledge that we do not know for how long, and to what degree, the changes in Ms A would be sustained. I accept that to establish such things, one needs evidence from follow-up. The second part of my response is to point out that there were convergent lines of evidence in the present, not only from Ms A's behavior and mood state and from the sessions themselves, but also from Ms A's own testimony, to the effect that the treatment was helpful.

The third part of my response is perhaps more subtle, but in my view most important. This is to argue that the step-by-step evolution of treatment might be taken to depict not only *that* things changed, but also the nature of the developmental process involved. I hope the vignette has illustrated as much, and has conveyed how patient–therapist exchanges were directly related to shifts in Ms A's ways of thinking and feeling about herself.

Here I would add something further that pertains specifically to Ms A, but is also relevant for other patients. There is one sense in which Ms A changed a lot. There is another sense in which the changes were modest. Ms A became what she had already the potential to become, even as she entered treatment. The process drew on and enhanced Ms A's strengths. It enabled her to deploy her resources in new ways, and make fresh choices as to how she would conduct her emotional life. Treatment of patients who have fewer resources is unlikely to take a course such as this.

To some readers it will be no surprise that benefit can come from brief psychotherapy, but it is a point seldom made in relation to brief treatment working on *psychoanalytic* principles. Of course, a single case history only suggests that the treatment might have value, and it remains to establish for how many people this is the case.

A theme to which we shall often return is that much of the therapeutic work is concerned with understanding and addressing moment-by-moment goings-on between patient and therapist. This is not to neglect what is happening *within* the patient's mind, of course. On the contrary, the approach is founded on the conviction that there is a close developmental relation between intrapsychic and interpersonal modes of relatedness. Roles and attitudes that a patient assumes and/or imposes in relation to other people—and in particular, the person of the therapist—reflect roles and attitudes the patient tends to adopt towards him/herself. If one understands and gains a purchase on what is happening *between* patient and therapist, then one has an opportunity to change what happens within a patient's mind.

I hope it is evident how much attention I devoted to Ms A's own active involvement in creating, sustaining, and sometimes imposing unfulfilling (or as time went on, increasingly fulfilling) patterns of engagement and/or defense. Inevitably and appropriately, this meant that time was spent tracing how Ms A's anxieties or other feelings were being dealt with, albeit at a high cost, through her struggles to maintain a manageable equilibrium. Although it was not clear how far Ms A was aware of playing such a major role in generating her own unhappy state at the time she sought treatment, soon she came to see that at least to some extent, she was exercising choice in taking up this or that stance in relation to herself and others.

A prime concern of Brief Psychoanalytic Therapy is to enhance the scope and strength of a person's grip on his or her mental and emotional life. The patient needs to become aware of the implications of choosing this or that path, moment by moment. In the end, it is the patient's decision which of the available options to take.

Concluding discussion

I trust this chapter has given a flavor of some important features of Brief Psychoanalytic Therapy. The clinical vignette was condensed, and contained little information about Ms A's past history or current life. In part, as in other cases presented in the book, this was attributable to the need to maintain confidentiality. It was also a reflection of what I consider most important for, and in some ways most characteristic of, Brief Psychoanalytic Therapy. Although in the case described, time was spent on addressing links between Ms A's experiences and her past and present relationships, such efforts were not central to the therapy. Important, yes, but not central.

The principal focus in Brief Psychoanalytic Therapy is what is happening now within sessions, between patient and therapist. True, understanding what is happening now is much enriched by knowledge of the patient's other intimate relationships, whether with parents or other caregivers, offspring, or current partners and colleagues. Ms A's associations to such relationships were very revealing, and they contributed to deeper understanding of her emotional predicament. Yet rarely did the ability to track here-and-now patient–therapist transactions depend on such information.

From a complementary perspective, it may be questioned to what extent a patient needs to be helped to see links between the past and present to benefit from psychotherapy. Some therapists believe that the creation of a meaningful narrative that makes sense of a person's life is one of the prime aims of psychotherapy. I am skeptical of such a view, especially when it is accompanied by a relatively laissez-faire attitude to how the narrative is constructed, and a relative disdain for the quest for what is true of the patient.

I think that the search for what is true is at the heart of psychotherapy. I also think that often reconstruction of past events or even plausible links among various figures in a person's life are more than a little speculative. After all, these figures are not literally present in the consulting room. Therefore my prime focus is on what *is* literally present and potentially available to patient and therapist alike (Feldman 2009). When a patient has the experience of being understood by someone firmly as well as compassionately seeking after the truth of how the patient is conducting his or her emotional life *in the session*, then this amounts to a powerful factor promoting integration and change.

Chapter 4

A second case history

Introduction

This chapter is devoted to a second case description. Here I focus on the initial assessment interview and then the final session of psychotherapy. My aim is to bring into relief how the patient's ways of thinking and feeling, and his manner of relating to himself and toward at least one person who had significance for him (in the form of a therapist), changed over the period of treatment. I shall dwell not on events in the patient's everyday life, although there were indications of significant shifts in his personal and professional dealings, but on his orientation toward his own conduct and feelings.

This patient, Mr. B, was seen by myself for the initial assessment consultation. Following this, he was taken on for treatment by a senior female trainee whose work I supervised. The therapist has kindly allowed me to quote from her written notes on the process of the final session.

In my view, details of this final session reveal the therapist's contribution in helping Mr. B to think about rather than push away feelings, and make use of his own insights in order to develop and grow. We see how the therapist's steadiness and gentle firmness, rooted in her compassion and respect for Mr. B, established an interpersonal relationship in which the patient could find the courage and ability to address what he had previously kept at bay. It was only once Mr. B had begun to make his first, faltering steps toward change with the help of his therapist, that he could begin to change within his own mind—and even then with hesitation and a lot of mixed feelings.

It is not unusual for a seemingly simple but critically important theme to emerge over the course of Brief Psychoanalytic Therapy. This can presage a period when the patient has a fierce struggle—again, both between the therapist and him/herself, and within his/her own mind—to make sense of what this means from an emotional vantage point. It was only slowly that Mr. B's intellectual half-understanding deepened into more personal and committed insight. As is often the case, there were back-and-forth movements between Mr. B's genuine and painful acknowledgment, and a half-dismissing state of mind. In the case of Mr. B, the issue was whether he could and would think.

Case vignette

Mr. B was a 35-year-old man referred by a psychiatrist for the reason that he was finding it difficult to sustain his attendance at courses required for his mature student training as an architect. The psychiatrist considered that Mr. B was suffering from generalized anxiety disorder with elements of social phobia and periodic depression. He was said to be worrying much of the time and finding it difficult to maintain intimate relationships. Mr. B had done well at school, but found it difficult to apply himself at university and had subsequently taken a number of casual jobs. In his early thirties he re-sat some exams and was accepted for training as an architect.

Mr. B had been sent a questionnaire about himself well before his initial consultation interview, and he returned this shortly before the interview itself. I shall not detail Mr. B's difficult childhood history. He was currently in a long-term but somewhat distanced relationship with a woman.

The initial consultation

When I met Mr. B at the time of his assessment consultation, he presented as a thin youthful looking man, hail fellow well met in manner. He said he did not know where to begin, perhaps I would like to ask him questions. Clearly he felt unsettled and put out that I was not taking a lead in shaping the interview. When we returned to this issue later in the meeting, it turned out that he had felt resentful and resistant, feelings that remained throughout our interview. However, Mr. B dealt with the situation by giving a fluent but superficial account of the events in his life over recent years, and described how he has had difficulties because of what his psychiatrist calls anxiety. He said he does worry a lot, He has periods of low motivation, and sometimes withdraws.

I took up how Mr. B's description of himself, although articulate and fluent, was pitched at a certain level. It seemed to involve an account of how happenings interfered with his progress. Mr. B edgily defended himself, and said he was just trying to give a picture.

Even this early on in the meeting, a pattern was becoming established that was to recur repeatedly in the course of the consultation. As Mr. B came to describe in detail, he is extremely proud and sensitive in relation to what others think about him. Here with me, he felt judged negatively, put on the spot, and found wanting. He said that already in this meeting, he had become resistant to the process and guarded in everything he said.

I acknowledged that this was how he felt, and how he had responded to the way he felt treated by me. At the same time, I persisted in pointing out how, rather than relating to himself as having vulnerabilities or neediness—and notwithstanding his genuine wish for help—he tended to present himself in a matter-of-fact way. It was very difficult to get access to anything personal about him.

It was only because I sustained a focus on Mr. B's need to protect himself that he became willing to divulge that he can be very frustrated, denigrating, intolerant, and unhappy about things in himself that he wishes were different. After considerable work in our exchanges, he came to speak of his self-destructiveness, competitiveness, and feelings of wishing to be the best; his mix of being very vulnerable and a worrier and yet well able to fight his corner; and most important of all, his difficulty in seeking help or allowing access to his feelings when he is not in control.

It also became apparent that Mr. B took a kind of pride in the fact that he hides things from other people. One of the issues I tried to take up was how honest he was, not least with himself. Repeatedly, he would raise emotional issues but describe them so that they were not accessible for us to take seriously. At least a part of this seemed to express Mr. B's determination to keep me at bay and to keep himself at least one step back from direct engagement. This was also reflected in Mr. B's difficulty in hearing me whenever I made a positive remark about him. I took up how, when I pinpointed something happening in relation to myself, he was mostly able to acknowledge the truth about himself. At such times he appeared to be able to make use of what I had said, and (I thought) show some relief, yet it was not clear whether he could allow this to take.

When toward the end of the interview, I asked Mr. B where he felt he was now, he said: "Do you want me to be honest?!" Then he said he really didn't like this at all. Mainly he felt I was criticizing him. Actually, he felt it was unfair that I expected him to come in here and be personal, especially in such a short time. He was quite explicit that yes, much of what I had said was perfectly true. And yes, he knows that this is important. But he just wants to feel better, and he is not especially keen to pursue the truth about himself, except as a means to that end.

As Mr. B emphasized more than once, he has had to look after himself from childhood, and that is what he feels he needs to do now. I said that this seems to be at the expense of feelings that never properly get addressed, either by himself or with anyone else. But if he were really to register this—and I said that at some level, I think he does—he is not going to allow that to be a shared recognition.

I might add that in all this, I felt I was treading a fine line. On the one hand, Mr. B realized that he needed to be challenged over the more controlling, attacking side to his personality. On the other hand, he could easily feel any challenge as criticism, and he was open about how sensitive he is to what others think of him and how prone he is to hide things or run away.

I asked Mr. B whether he dreams. He could remember one dream, only sketchily. There were classmates at school whom he did not like anyway, who were rejecting him. Initially he kept this dream at arms' length, effectively rejecting my obvious wish to understand something about him through the dream. When I brought him back to the content of the dream, he flushed and said that obviously the feelings were not nice. Again he made it clear how reluctant he was to engage with a matter of emotional significance. The content of the dream included a clear indication of how he was prone to lessen the pain of rejection by diminishing his own vulnerability (he did not like the classmates anyway), and in relation to myself, too, he made sure he was protected so that if anyone was going to experience rejection, it was myself.

I said to Mr. B that we might be able to revisit and think over some of the issues we had addressed, in a further meeting. I said I felt he was pessimistic about change; no doubt he has reasons for his investment in keeping control in the way he does. I said I really was uncertain myself whether he could, or would choose to, commit himself to the process of psychotherapy in such a way that he could develop. But I said I thought he had underlying insights into himself, and knows that his potential for self-defeating behavior puts him at real risk professionally.

I said it would not help if I were to recommend what he does. I stressed he would need to sign up for treatment if this were to happen. I also mentioned alternative treatment options, and he said he would go away and think about it.

My lack of a recommendation was not an expression of lack of concern. On the contrary, I had a sincere wish for Mr. B to become engaged in dynamic psychotherapy. The problem was that I was also sincere in my expressions of doubt about his commitment. Given Mr. B's negative feelings toward myself and his intense ambivalence toward dependency, there was a risk that if I gave advice, this might militate against what I advised. Just as important, I felt that if Mr. B *could* use the events of our meeting in a positive way, and summon the commitment to embark on treatment, this would give him an optimal, and perhaps much-needed, basis for seeing through what I anticipated would be a fraught and perhaps fragile psychotherapy with an uncertain outcome.

I would like to add a few additional remarks about the assessment consultation. Recall how the psychiatrist had referred Mr. B for "generalized anxiety disorder with elements of social phobia and periodic depression." In the context of the assessment consultation, as Mr. B's states of mind unfolded in the relatively stressful context of our interpersonal contact, the nature of his anxieties, the fears that attended personal engagement, and aspects of his unhappiness and pessimism came to assume more specific form. Some psychiatrists and psychologists would consider that the initial diagnostic categories should retain their status as indicators of effective therapeutic remedies for Mr. B. I am inclined to a different view, namely, that in the absence of supportive evidence such as unexplained features of biological depression, psychiatric diagnoses had served their purpose as preliminary descriptive terms and could now be superseded as a more specific characterization of Mr. B's difficulties became available.

There is much that remains unknown after an assessment consultation. I consider this to have been a revealing interview, but one that left a lot to be discovered. I had gained a relatively clear view of Mr. B's vulnerabilities and strengths, a sense of his range of emotional experience and expressiveness, and a tentative grasp of his difficulties in allowing intimate engagement as well as his self-protective moves to insulate himself from the dangers of dependency. My prime source of knowledge, of course, was what had occurred in relation to myself in the transference, and my own countertransference experiences. But how far should I believe Mr. B when he said he was not keen to pursue the truth about himself? What I felt I could not judge was how the balance of forces toward deeper engagement on the one hand, or withdrawal and rejection of a therapist on the other, would tilt in the psychotherapy process. And that, I felt, depended on the sensitivity and skill of the therapist as well as on Mr. B himself.

The course of psychotherapy

In the event, Mr. B took up the option to enter Brief Psychoanalytic Therapy. Not unexpectedly, treatment proved to be a choppy process. In the sessions with his female trainee psychotherapist, he often came late, and sometimes cancelled.

Mr. B was especially disturbed by the fact that he was required to take some responsibility for what was happening, and experienced the therapist as persecuting. He found it profoundly unsettling when the therapist pointed out how his actions were governed by his thinking. He was adamant that no thinking went into his actions; to think meant to be responsible and he would not be held responsible for things out of his control. He parried interpretations of what he was doing by saying he didn't do things on purpose, and protested that he felt lost and confused—as indeed, he did. Moreover, he insisted he could not ask for help, and said in so many words that it would be stupid to let the therapist affect him emotionally. As the therapist recorded: "Short of walking out and completely disengaging, Mr. B tried everything to remain distant and unengaged."

However, there were also indications of change. Mr. B began to remark on how he needed to try to make use of psychotherapy; he realized he undermines it. He recognized how he can go round in circles in a sterile way. A condensed account of the final session of the psychotherapy should serve to illustrate both Mr. B's tendency to push away, especially at the beginning of a meeting, and his growing potential to allow personal contact.

The final session

Mr. B arrived 15 minutes late. He started the session by giving explanations for his lateness. He said he was feeling very unwell. He had taken some antibiotics and perhaps they didn't agree with him. He was late starting because his class ran over. And on reaching here he had to go to the toilet first, his stomach was upset. The therapist said that perhaps his lateness might also be due to the fact that this was their last session. Irritated, Mr. B said that wasn't the case at all. These were just coincidences and he could never understand the connections the therapist made. What possible connection could an upset stomach have to do with the last session?

The therapist said yes, Mr. B has mentioned before that what is difficult or painful to think about, he prefers not to consider at all. Mr. B retorted: "Fine, whatever you say." He added that he is really not in a condition to think today. There was a period of quiet. He said that he hoped until the last minute that he would reach the session on time. The therapist said that he had flushed all the upset out of his system.

After a further quiet, Mr. B said: "OK, so you are saying that's what made me anxious. The therapy ending. This anxious. Maybe it did. But I don't think so. I don't get anxious like this." Both therapist and patient were again quiet.

Mr. B said: "OK, I know I get anxious but I was certainly not anxious about getting here late. Why would I? What am I going to achieve in the last session?" After a brief silence, the therapist said how Mr. B was upset in the previous session also. He had said how the ending felt so uncontained.

Mr. B said: "I don't know. These sessions have made no sense to me whatsoever. I don't know what I am expected to do with them. They stay with me for a day or two but then I have to get on with life. There is a lot to do. I don't know how these sessions will help. I don't understand them." The therapist said perhaps the problem right now is thinking about the ending with her. Mr. B said he didn't want to think. He doesn't believe in mulling over things. He believes in taking action. Thinking should be a reflex action.

After a silence, Mr. B said: "OK, maybe not a reflex." He continued that maybe he was thinking but he doesn't do it consciously. He *is* doing much better now in terms of handling his life and his affairs. He is not running away from things. His girlfriend thinks he has improved. He doesn't know why. Maybe because this time she actually saw him revising and getting up on time and not missing classes … Oh, yes, they have decided to move in together. End of the month, they are taking a flat together. He said he was very happy they are able to do that.

The therapist said that despite this, Mr. B did not want to take the credit that as a thinking being, he is responsible for these changes. He was quiet, and then said: "You *force* me to think in these sessions. You can't expect me to do that on my own. There is so much to do this year. I can't just sit and think." The therapist said that he feels he cannot do on his own what he has been able to achieve in these sessions, with her help. He feels that she is leaving him and now telling him to grow up and handle life himself. He was quiet, and then said "Maybe." But he doesn't want to think.

After remarking that he had never seen any treatment through to the end, Mr. B said that his therapist had mentioned a few times that he felt he has been offered short-term therapy because it suited the therapist's needs—and he had indeed thought that. But he didn't think so now because he had been the one cancelling and she the one rescheduling. The therapist said it was important for Mr. B to know that she thought he was important enough for appointments to be rescheduled. It was important for him to know that she cared.

After another brief silence, Mr. B said: "It's difficult to do this by oneself. If there is someone holding your hand you can do it, but to do it on your own … all this thinking. It's very scary. I know that I can sabotage it all. But also maybe it will be impossible to not think now. Only time will tell whether this will stay or I will go back to square one. But it's me who stops it from happening." He went on to talk about difficulties in trusting himself as well as others. He has always hated himself and so he believes others hate him. And if that is what you think then it is best not to think, and to keep yourself separate from others. He has thought a certain way for so many years, how will 16 hours of therapy change that?

The therapist said that Mr. B was asking her why she would encourage him to develop trust and start having a relationship with her, only to tell him it has now ended. She is like the antibiotic that leaves him sicker. After a pause, he said that what he can do in these sessions, he may not be able to do outside. The sessions are different. The therapist said that he had always maintained that the sessions were in some way artificial and disconnected from real life. He said yes, after all, he doesn't meet other people every week for 16 hours. Unable to stop herself, the therapist said he meets other people every day! He was quiet, then smiled, and said: "Yeah. I meant that the way I am able to speak and think here, I can't with other people."

The therapist said that he has allowed himself to trust her in these sessions, despite it being so difficult for him. Though he believed she thought ill of him, and often experienced her as hostile, he still gave the relationship a second chance. He said quietly: "That's exactly what I wouldn't have done earlier." After a pause, the therapist said he has started a process here, a way of relating to himself and others, but he fears that he will react to the end by sabotaging it. Mr. B nodded quietly and said he will try not to do that. Here the final session ended.

Some months later, Mr. B arranged to pick up the threads by embarking on longer-term psychotherapy elsewhere.

Discussion

I cannot know what effect this account may have on readers, but I find it both sad and uplifting. The delicacy of the means by which Mr. B communicated his state, and the sensitivity with which the therapist allowed Mr. B to move slowly from prickly defensiveness to serious acknowledgment and shared insight, are testament to the specialness of psychoanalytic psychotherapy.

The changes that took place over the course of this final session reflected and in a way recapitulated the changes that had been taking place over the course of the treatment. The patient had missed sessions and often come late. Over periods of weeks, the therapist had had to manage frustration, yearning, self-doubt, and anxiety about the continuance and outcome of treatment, as well as feelings of rejection, dejection, and near-hopelessness. Yet her hope and belief survived, and her therapeutic attitude was enhanced rather than weakened by the experience. In learning about this final session, we gain a sense of how the therapist believed the patient himself could (with her support) manage more by way of reflection and interpersonal contact than had at first seemed the case.

All this illustrates what it means for a therapist to contain feelings in the countertransference. Much of what the therapist had to experience was induced by Mr. B's behavior toward her. Sometimes it was she who suffered states of distress or aggressiveness that Mr. B needed her to experience, when he himself either could not feel and/or could not contain them. She was able to register the feelings, to express them in supervision, and respond to them not by retaliation nor by unrealistic calmness but by understanding the need to address them within herself and within the relationship with Mr. B.

I would stress two things about all this. Firstly, the limits of what a patient can achieve are often set by the limits of what a therapist can manage. I am not surprised that this very able therapist enabled this patient to develop as far as he did. One way in which psychoanalysts envisage the developmental process is to consider how a patient such as Mr. B needs to project unmanageable states of mind into the mind of the therapist. If the therapist can contain and assimilate those states, the patient can take back ownership of the states of mind, now in more manageable form. In fact, processes akin to these find expression in the manifest to-and-fro of the final session with Mr. B.

Secondly, and related to this, I think we can see how what was achieved *between* the therapist and Mr. B bore a close relation to what was achieved within Mr. B's own mind. Mr. B himself states this explicitly, and avows more than once that it is one thing for him to think in the therapist's presence, but another for him to do this by himself, even though he knows there has been development in that respect. He seems perfectly aware that modes of thought and feeling had become new options for him, in virtue of their emergence in the context of his relationship with the therapist. More than this, his experience was that she had forced him to think. The therapist was firm as well as understanding. At the same time, through her sensitivity to the anxieties and threats that made thinking so hazardous for Mr. B, she enabled him to become a person with the courage to think in the face of perils and pain.

My next point is that although many of this therapist's interventions do, as a matter of fact, conform with the principles of Brief Psychoanalytic Therapy to be laid out in ensuing chapters, there is no sense that she is following instructions or acting in accordance with rules. Indeed, one of the most important and impressive things about the session is the degree to which she *refrains* from commenting or interpreting, but trusts that Mr. B will move forward by himself. It would have been easy for a therapist to have short-circuited this development. Such periods were not, as it were, just silences, because they often occurred when Mr. B had expressed skepticism and even dismissiveness toward the therapist's views. Her quiet response conveyed something hugely important about her willingness to accept the patient's position and the way he treated her. At the same time, she would go on believing what she had good reason to see as the most significant and emotionally alive issues in the session, and to remark on these as and when it seemed Mr. B might be able to hear.

As it turned out, Mr. B's own movement suggests he was hearing the therapist from the very beginning, and had perhaps anticipated her orientation even before the session began. The critical thing here is that the therapist's attitude influenced Mr. B in a way that seemed neither forced nor superficial. By the end of this session, Mr. B's statements carried conviction and had emotional depth.

There is another way of looking at the relation between a therapist's emotional stance and his or her technique. I stated in an earlier chapter that technique is worse than useless without understanding imbued with feeling. What one is aiming for is to evolve a technique that expresses, reflects, and refines a therapist's sensitivity and effectiveness in coming to understand and communicate that understanding to a patient. In reading the therapist's account of her final session with Mr. B, for me it is the therapist's emotional presence and deftness of communication that impresses most deeply. It is only as a subsidiary matter that I marvel at her technical skills. This is as it should be.

Yet I have a counter-reaction to what I have just written. It assumes too much. It so happens that this therapist and I share an orientation to psychoanalytic psychotherapy, and for this reason I can take for granted the underpinnings of her approach. Centrally, this therapist knows what it is to work in the transference. She is attentive to her patient's implicit as well as explicit communications toward herself. She is alert not only to his ways of protecting himself, both from psychic pain and conflict and from the dangers of interpersonal engagement, but also to his underlying fears, anxieties, and potentially destructive feelings such as envy. Therefore it is through a particular set of understandings and interventions that her emotional presence and deftness of communication is expressed. There really is not an either/or here. A therapist who had technical skills but no heart would not have the requisite therapeutic skill at all, but a therapist who had heart but no intellectual nor technical skills might well feel at a loss how to proceed.

At this point I would like to review aspects of the final session, and in particular, emphasize the simplicity and directness of some of the therapist's statements. What they express is deep, and the way they are expressed, especially in the face of Mr. B's seeming efforts to push weighty matters to one side, is correspondingly serious. Very early on in the session, as well as later, the therapist makes reference to the impending end of the treatment. She is well aware of the significance of this for Mr. B, and he is left in no doubt about it. It does not take long before he, too, reflects on some of the implications of his ending their joint work. Then when Mr. B protests, the therapist refers to the recurrent issue of Mr. B's difficulty in thinking rather than flushing things away. She also raises the more specific matter of his upset in the last session. Clearly she is holding the patient and the therapy in mind. Her remarks do not move away from the present, rather they enrich its meaning. Then she acknowledges both his actually having tolerated thinking, and his reluctance to take responsibility for this achievement.

Soon afterwards, the therapist states with clarity and lack of fuss how Mr. B has needed to know that she cares. What followed (as recalled by the therapist) deserves quoting again in full:

> Mr. B said: "It's difficult to do this by oneself. If there is someone holding your hand you can do it, but to do it on your own … all this thinking. It's very scary. I know that I can sabotage it all. But also maybe it will be impossible to not think now. Only time will tell whether this will stay or I will go back to square one. But it's me who stops it from happening." He went on to talk about difficulties in trusting himself as well as others. He has always hated himself and so he believes others hate him. And if that is what you think then it is best not to think, and to keep yourself separate from others. He has thought a certain way for so many years, how will 16 hours of therapy change that?

This is an extraordinarily condensed account of some central features of Mr. B's emotional life. But of course, it is not just an abstract account, it is Mr. B's communication to his therapist, someone who he knows will listen carefully and take what he says seriously. This communication is part and parcel of the process through which Mr. B, too, is coming to take seriously what he says and thinks. It is also part and parcel of his experiencing trust. He communicates not only his vulnerability but also his responsibility for sabotage and allows this to be seen and shared.

These exchanges led to the final few moments of the session, when both patient and therapist were able to integrate positive and negative experiences of the therapy. Mr. B could even acknowledge the therapist's suggestion that he had managed to give the relationship a second chance, something he would (he said) have been unable to do previously.

In conclusion, I believe that in this therapist's capacity and willingness to bear difficult feelings in the countertransference and maintain her emotional availability and thoughtfulness on Mr. B's behalf, in her patience and courage to take risks in what she said, and in her sensitivity to the positive and negative sides of Mr. B's relatedness toward her—all anchored in the immediacy of her mutual engagement with Mr. B—she provided what he needed to develop through the stuckness of the mindset with which he sought treatment. It came as welcome news that subsequently, Mr. B was intending to build on what he had achieved, in seeking further longer-term psychotherapy.

A final thought about Mr. B. One of the tasks of conducting an assessment consultation, is to evaluate whether or not a particular patient will find psychotherapy destabilizing in an unhelpful way, or whether he or she will weather inevitable disturbance and discover more fruitful ways to live. There was sufficient indication in my consultation with Mr. B that he had strengths on which he could draw. Just as importantly, he could use the help of a therapist, even one toward whom he had understandable ambivalence. It turned out that in treatment, too, despite his feelings of being unloved or even hated and his own resentment at being forced to think, and despite his own nearly successful but ultimately half-hearted acts of sabotage, Mr. B could hear and respect emotional truths about himself, and make those truths his own.

Of course, it had been reasonable for Mr. B to question how 16 sessions could possibly change deeply ingrained patterns of thinking and feeling. And yet ...

Chapter 5

The Treatment Manual

Introduction

It is time to lay out the principles of Brief Psychoanalytic Therapy, in the form of a Treatment Manual. A treatment manual is supposed to convey the essentials of a given treatment. When I circulated this Manual to potential therapists, I added two illustrative clinical vignettes from a previous book of mine (Hobson 2002/2004, *The Cradle of Thought*). I omit these here, in the expectation that the fresh clinical material contained in other chapters will more than suffice to illustrate how the Manual can be applied. Given that the Manual amounts to a distillation, I trust readers will bear with me if sections recapitulate themes already introduced in earlier chapters. Because the Manual is intended to be self-contained, I make it clear where it begins and ends.

At the time I wrote the Manual, the readers I had in mind were psychiatrists, clinical psychologists, social workers, and nurses who had substantial theoretical and practical knowledge of psychoanalytic psychotherapy. Re-reading the Manual now, I see that some sections might need explanation or elaboration for a broader audience. Rather than meddle with the text, which I would like to keep as succinct as possible, I have chosen to supplement the Manual with an Appendix in which I revisit the opening of my assessment consultation with Ms A (Chapter 3). I trust this will clarify some potential obscurities, and begin to flesh out what a Brief Psychoanalytic orientation means in practice.

This Treatment Manual and the Adherence Manual (Chapter 7) complement one another. In effect, the Adherence Manual is an applied version of the Treatment Manual, exemplifying how the principles of treatment find expression in what a therapist actually says and does in treatment. From a complementary perspective, what a therapist says and does is expressive of the therapist's thinking and feeling, as well as indicative of what the therapist believes will be helpful to the patient. The Adherence Manual lays out a series of therapeutic strategies, but these need to implicate something deeper, namely the therapist's involvement with and understanding of the patient on a personal level. The Treatment Manual points to what such involvement and understanding entail.

Brief Psychoanalytic Therapy Treatment Manual

This Manual is almost exclusively concerned to characterize the features of technique that are special (albeit not exclusive) to Brief Psychoanalytic Therapy (BPT). The intention is not to prescribe what a therapist should do, but rather to convey the principles according to which a BPT therapist works, and to illustrate how these principles are likely to find expression in the minutiae of therapist–patient interactions.

The Manual is in two parts, as follows:

Part 1: After a brief introduction, I provide the rationale for and principles of BPT. Subsequently, I detail therapeutic strategies a therapist might employ.

Part 2: I focus in more detail, with examples, on giving in-transference interpretations (material largely abstracted from Hobson and Kapur 2005). I discuss the anchorage, focus, and style of such interpretations. Briefly, I reflect on the course of psychotherapy.

Part 1: The principles of Brief Psychoanalytic Therapy

Introduction

Brief Psychoanalytic Therapy (BPT) is a specific form of short-term psychodynamic psychotherapy 16 sessions in duration. It is distinguished from other forms of brief psychotherapy in two respects, although each of these is largely a matter of degree: (a) there is a relatively restricted focus upon the transference relationship between therapist and patient, so that the approach amounts to focal psychotherapy of a particular kind, and (b) the setting is managed, and the therapeutic interventions are framed, in specific ways that accord with the aim of helping the patient re-integrate aspects of his/her emotional life. It is distinguished from some forms of longer-term psychoanalytic psychotherapy not only by its brevity, but also by a quality of intense attention to the transference and countertransference that might be contrasted with a therapeutic attitude intended to facilitate the unfolding of the transference over weeks or months, or an approach that gives priority to reconstruction of a patient's history.

Brief Psychoanalytic Therapy is rooted in psychoanalytic theory and practice. However, this does not mean that practitioners of the approach need to have had full psychoanalytic training, helpful though this would be. Nor does it require allegiance to many of the ideas that form the body of psychoanalytic thinking. What it does mean is that therapists need to be able to apprehend and understand the transference, that is, the qualities of relatedness that a patient brings to bear in his/her relationship with the therapist, and the kinds of involvement that the patient engenders in the psychotherapist. This requires that the psychotherapist is able to monitor and understand his/her countertransference to the patient, and to formulate his/her understandings of what is happening in ways that are accessible to, and helpful for, the patient. These are no small matters. In practice, they entail that a psychotherapist will need to have had (and in the course of therapy, continue to have access to) training and supervision.

Rationale

There are two overriding principles to the thinking behind BPT:

1. Given an appropriate setting, a patient will engage with a psychotherapist in such a way as to introduce patterns of relatedness and relationship that are not only characteristic of the patient, but also an important source of the patient's presenting problems.

2. If a psychotherapist is able to respond to—and when indicated, express understanding of—these patterns of relatedness and relationship in appropriate ways, then this may promote development and change in the patient.

The rationale for these principles is founded on two empirical claims. The first claim is that people repeat patterns of relatedness and relationship, not only with other significant people but also within themselves. The second claim is that if a psychotherapist whom a patient implicates in such repeating patterns offers emotional understanding and containment, then often, but not always, changes in those patterns can be effected.

The first claim involves the idea that there is an intimate connection between what goes on *between* people, and what goes on *within* a person's mind—where each of these goings-on tend to be repetitive and therefore a feature of a person's personality—and the second extends this notion to encompass a developmental perspective. Although the most original and important source of thinking about each principle is Freud (especially Freud's 1917 paper on Mourning and Melancholia) and object relations writers who elaborated his ideas such as Fairbairn (1952), Klein (e.g., 1975b, originally 1957), Winnicott (1965a,b), and Bion (1962a, 1967), related perspectives are part of the mainstream of developmental psychology (especially Vygotsky 1978).

Critical here is the notion that an individual has a propensity to identify with the attitudes of another significant person (as experienced). In so doing, the individual assimilates from the other person the potential to adopt those attitudes either toward other people, or toward him/herself. This means that what begins as a quality of relatedness in the interpersonal domain can enter a patient's mental repertoire. The idea has importance *both* for understanding the genesis of personality and psychopathology *and* for the mechanisms of therapeutic change. In the latter respect, there is an opportunity for a patient to re-integrate aspects of his/her emotional life and personality through his/her relationship with a psychotherapist, and, more specifically, to acquire new capacities to tolerate and think about difficult states of mind through the psychotherapist's capacity to encompass and think about the patient's patterns of relatedness in treatment.

There are important complexities to this seemingly simple picture, however. In particular, the significant person (as experienced) will be colored by what someone projects on to the person, or, according to Kleinian theory, locates in the other through projective identification. Therefore what the patient takes in as a grounding for fresh developments in emotional regulation may not be so fresh after all. Moreover, the qualities and contents of such projections may be affected by the developmental level on which a person is functioning, as well as his/her psychopathology.

An implication is that a psychotherapist requires special sensitivity and skill to frame his/her understanding so that, instead of merely repeating experiences in the therapeutic relationship, a patient registers (although does not necessarily acknowledge) that something new is being provided. The source of the something new is the therapist's capacity to recognize and encompass the patient's difficult-to-bear states of mind. Such states of mind might be suffused with anxiety, aggression, sexual desire, envy, or a myriad of other attitudes and feelings.

Principles of treatment

The first principle of treatment is that the psychotherapist has a focus on the ways in which a patient relates to the psychotherapist him/herself. More specifically, the task of the psychotherapist is to discern how the patient presents him/herself as someone to be related to in particular ways. Often a patient tries to provide a script for how the therapist should behave so that certain difficulties or conflicts are avoided, and shapes his/her own role in order to establish and maintain emotional equilibrium. For example, it is not uncommon for patients to put themselves in the hands of the psychotherapist as the expert, and to anticipate that their role is simply to answer the therapist's questions and receive advice in exchange, rather than think for themselves. Sometimes it seems as if the capacity to think about things, and to address matters squarely, is ascribed to the therapist in such a way that no-one could expect the patient to have thoughts about the nature and sources of his/her difficulties. Alternatively, there are patients who seek to excise or otherwise rid themselves of this or that aspect of their feelings or personality, either by requesting to be cured of their problem, or by subtly relocating what they cannot manage so that it has to be borne by the therapist.

The second principle is that a focus on the transference should be informed by the therapist's analysis of the countertransference, that is, the feelings that the therapist has or is inclined to have in relation to the patient. Sometimes, indeed, the therapist has to monitor his own actions and statements to discover how he/she is conforming to a role that is either shaped by the patient, or assumed by the therapist in response to what the patient induces in him/herself. For example, a therapist may find him/herself offering explanations of this or that feature of the patient's difficulties, in response to discomfort common to patient and therapist alike, namely that of being faced with incomprehensible and disturbing states of mind.

The third principle is that the psychotherapist's task is not only to understand how the patient is experiencing him/herself and the therapeutic setting (which may extend to the institution), but also to determine the patient's role in shaping the interpersonal exchanges within psychotherapy. Among other things, the psychotherapist will need to recognize what the patient does to deflect from or otherwise evade conflictual or aversive states of mind. Often this means discerning how the patient deploys defensive strategies, as these are enacted between patient and therapist as well as within the patient's own mind. Beyond this, the therapist will try to determine what particular anxieties, feeling states, or mode of relatedness underlie the patient's need for self-protection.

It may seem that to assume this focus on the transference and countertransference is to sideline or downplay a patient's manifest problems, complaints, and preoccupations, and/or marginalize important expressions of the patient's difficulties in and beyond current relationships and life activities, and/or minimize attention to important sources of current psychopathology in the patient's significant relationships from early in life. This should not be the case at all, for at least two reasons. Firstly, the psychotherapist is aware of the importance of these matters, and is free to prompt a patient to talk about them if they are not raised and described spontaneously. Indeed, a psychotherapist might well express his/her belief that the patterns that emerge in therapy are probably familiar to the patient, and not merely restricted to the current therapeutic relationship. Secondly, the patient will very often raise such matters spontaneously, in the context of understandings that emerge in the transference. Far from being treated as peripheral, these links are allowed to enrich and amplify the process and progress of treatment.

The point is not that the transference, and only the transference, matters. To the contrary, it is the person's life that matters. Rather, it is within the transference that central emotional and relational conflicts and anxieties become immediately apparent and amenable to change. It is through the patient as well as therapist experiencing, reflecting upon, and understanding the transference that other aspects of the patient's life become more comprehensible and available for revision.

Therapeutic strategies

The conduct of psychotherapy is managed to optimize the likelihood of developmental change in relevant aspects of the patient's emotional/relational life. Such change has interpersonal and intra-psychic aspects.

There are two principles here. Firstly, the therapist needs to arrange a therapeutic setting that allows a patient's characteristic relatedness patterns to become manifest. Secondly, the therapist needs to be in a position to register and think about the patient–therapist transactions in a way that both contains the patient's (and the therapist's) emotional states without undue acting out and at the same time, to convey to the patient that degree of therapist understanding which is (a) justified, i.e., for which there is evidence present in the current patient–therapist transactions, and (b) assimilable by the patient. In this latter respect, clinical sensitivity is critical; it is worse than useless to bombard the patient, or to utter platitudes that are intended to be reassuring, or to offer nothing—although sometimes silence of the appropriate kind may communicate genuine understanding, not least in cases where to say anything would be to convey the therapist's intolerance of living with uncertainty.

In relation to the setting, BPT requires a quiet room that will be secure from interruption, for sessions of agreed-upon length, probably either 50 minutes or an hour. It is the therapist's responsibility to be available to start on time, and to finish on time. If the patient is late, the time of ending remains the same; once the session times have been established, and the patient misses a session, then the session is not replaced unless rescheduling is possible in advance, or there are exceptional circumstances.

In order to conduct BPT, a therapist needs to feel at ease within his/her own mind, and confident in his/her approach. This is needed so that perturbations induced by the patient may be registered as such. Very often, the therapist needs supervision in order to achieve and sustain this stance, as treatment proceeds.

The therapist's aim is to limit, as far as possible and reasonable, factors that will obscure the emergence of relatedness patterns that are particular to the patient. For example, if a therapist asks too many questions, this is likely to achieve little more than (a) revealing what the therapist thinks or needs or considers important, and (b) obscuring what the patient makes of the therapist's motives in asking the questions, and the stance the patient adopts in relation to what he/she supposes to be happening in the therapist. It is not that all questions are proscribed for the psychotherapist; of course not. Rather, questioning is sometimes less revealing or fruitful than allowing the patient to show what is pressing for the patient at a given moment. Similarly, it is often more helpful to respond to a patient's questions with responses that deepen contact, rather than either (a) answering directly, in which case, the meaning of the patient asking that question is often lost, or (b) parrying the question evasively. A firm and serious recognition of the importance of the question for the patient—and if needs be, a promise to return to the question later (a promise that will need to be fulfilled)—may be more productive. Alternatively, in those instances when a therapist has grounds for believing that the patient already has an answer, whether his/her own or what he/she anticipates from the therapist, it may be possible to draw the patient's attention to his actions (e.g., "You ask me"), perhaps with more specific elaboration (e.g., "I wonder if you have asked yourself," or, "You feel it should be me who addresses that … but perhaps it is something you know about").

So, too, it is rare for a therapist conducting BPT to offer advice, beyond advice to think over and take seriously what has emerged in the therapy, something that is already strongly implicit in the therapy itself. It is usually far more helpful to address how the patient is positioning him/herself, as one seemingly in need of advice from the therapist. Of course this is not to deny that a patient might need to be given advice from appropriate sources, for example in relation to taking medication.

So what is the therapist supposed to be saying and doing? He/she tries to provide understanding at those moments when the patient either needs first aid, when anxiety or conflict has become intolerable, or, more usually, when the patient had done or felt something in the therapeutic relationship which is:

- germane to treatment through its emotional significance;
- not something of which the patient is immediately aware; but
- something of which the patient can *become* aware through reflection on what has just happened between patient and therapist.

The approach is evidence-based, in the sense that for any intervention, there should be evidence available from which a patient—or indeed, a sensitive witness to the exchanges—could draw his/her own conclusions about the correctness or otherwise of what the therapist says.

A therapist, then, gives close attention to what the patient feels and does. This includes whatever the patient brings to the therapeutic situation to shape his/her experience of the therapist. For example, the therapist may need to state his belief that the patient is experiencing him as invasive or untrustworthy at a particular point in the interaction. The most telling evidence for what the patient is feeling or doing may come from the therapist's countertransference. Here, too, it should be the case that a witness who is in a position to identify with the therapist at any point in the exchanges is able to understand/ derive a similar countertransference response. In other words, there should be potential objectivity (through intersubjective agreement) as well as subjectivity in the evidence available.

A complication is that what a patient is doing and/or experiencing may depend upon the overarching qualities of his/her relational state at any moment of the therapy. Here one critical distinction derived from Kleinian theory is that between paranoid-schizoid and depressive position functioning (Klein 1975b, originally 1957). A person operating at the paranoid-schizoid level of functioning tends to experience threats to their own being, feelings of persecution and hostility from others, and a world peopled by unrealistically good or bad figures. Indeed, the experience is hardly of full, independent people at all, but rather, of people-like figures (part-objects) who have crudely configured-properties and functions e.g., to take awful states of mind away, or to feed, or to be hostile. A person operating in the depressive position, on the other hand, has a primary anxiety of losing a significant other, or losing the other person's love or positive regard, or harming the other, and there is a less nightmarish and more compassionate quality to the personal relations involved.

Paranoid-schizoid and depressive position functioning are by no means the only recognizable types of relatedness pattern, but they are among the most important. They matter for the stance that it may be appropriate for a therapist to take in offering understanding of a patient. For instance, it may be more effective to address what the patient experiences the therapist to be like, or to be doing or feeling, perhaps representing split-off and projected aspects of the patient's self, rather than to address what the patient is currently doing or feeling within him- or herself. Steiner (1993) has written about analyst-centred interpretations in this context. In addition, a therapist must respect how patients occupying a paranoid-schizoid world may be restricted by concrete and inflexible modes of thinking.

These different forms of functioning also matter for the aims of psychotherapy. With more troubled patients, one is seeking to promote integration of divided-up aspects of the personality. Although this aim is also relevant for patients who operate mostly in the depressive position, here it is often the case that therapy enables the patient to achieve a new understanding of what, as some level, they are already aware—to arrive where they started, and know the place for the first time.

A further aspect of the therapeutic relationship that requires close consideration from early in BPT is the significance of the ending of therapy. As in all forms of psychodynamic psychotherapy, much weight is given to a patient's experience of a dependent relationship with the therapist, and his/her reactions to separation and loss, with the highly ambivalent feelings these events can provoke. In BPT, it is important to attend to this from early in treatment, not only because it represents a point of distillation for central emotional/relational issues, but also because there is a need to anticipate responses to the ending of therapy that if unexplored might militate against the consolidation of gains. To consider this from a complementary perspective, the very intensity of BPT brings with it a therapeutic responsibility to help a patient deal with the real loss of the relationship within a relatively short span of time.

The course of psychotherapy

Psychotherapy has a beginning, a middle, and an end—as does each session. The importance of endings has already been highlighted. If all goes well, progress in psychotherapy will mean that emotional contact between patient and therapist will deepen and become increasingly subtle and flexible, and give rise to a sense of shared endeavor in facing psychic reality. In some patients, the balance between paranoid-schizoid and depressive position functioning will shift toward the latter, less disturbed state of mind, and/or the patient will acquire the ability to recover more quickly from phases in which the former state predominates. In other patients, there will emerge a greater tolerance of conflictual or otherwise unpleasant emotional states, a mitigation of self-critical judgment, and a freeing of emotional communication. In yet others, there will be a shift away from familiar self-protective but restricted modes of relating both to others and to the self, toward a willingness to be open to experience. In yet others, there will appear a new commitment and ability to think self-reflectively, rather than discharge feeling through action. And so on.

The common factor among these and other alternative patterns of change is that through the experience of psychotherapy—and, more specifically, through experience of a psychotherapist able to manage emotional states generated through the patient's own psychological difficulties—a patient becomes able to relate to him/herself and his/her emotional/relational states with less evasiveness and defensiveness, and to be emotionally available with others. All being well, this brings with it alleviation of the patient's presenting difficulties and distress, as well as enrichment of his or her personal life.

Thus far, this Manual has dealt with the principles and strategies of short-term psychoanalytic psychotherapy in a somewhat abstract manner. This is appropriate, insofar as the crux of the therapeutic approach is to follow principles and apply strategies sensitively and flexibly, rather than attempt to learn techniques by rote. Having said this, it may be helpful to focus upon a critical feature of the clinical work that exemplifies the principles already outlined, and that may benefit from further analysis and illustration: the psychotherapist's orientation in framing interpretations grounded in an understanding of the transference.

Part 2. In-transference interpretations

It is important that in order to understand the nature and force of transference interpretations, one appreciates the nature of the therapy within which interventions are made. In order to avoid unnecessary conflict with those who have argued for specific meanings to attach to the notion of transference interpretation, it is appropriate to provide a working definition of in-transference interpretations (see Hobson and Kapur 2005 for an empirical study of such interventions). In-transference interpretations elaborate on the here-and-now transactions between patient and therapist, viewed from the perspective of the patient's experience or the patient's role in shaping the exchanges.

An interpretation is defined as a comment by the therapist aimed to clarify the meaning(s) of the patient–therapist interaction that have just taken place. An in-transference interpretation comprises a therapist statement or group of statements that contains specific and direct reference to the therapist, usually containing the word "I" or "me," intended to clarify the patient's current feelings or actions in relation to the therapist. It is possible to achieve inter-rater reliability in identifying such interpretations in recorded interviews (Hobson and Kapur 2005). The following are examples taken from videotaped assessment consultations with different patients, and are intended to illustrate what actually happened in therapy, and *not* to represent models of ideal interpretations (which would be more succinct, for example):

- "You see how much you have to focus on what is in my mind. Immediately you focus on what I may have read [in a questionnaire] and registered and how I am going to help you. I don't know the motive for your need to know this but it's clear you need the spotlight on me, what I'm going to do, what I'm expecting, what I'm thinking, what I'm staring about, what I'm inquisitive about. The whole of your thought seems to be occupied with what's in my mind."

- "You see I think this goes very deep. In the questionnaire two of the things you mentioned, one was at one phase you had a, I don't know, a true problem with eating but also you said something about this peculiar business of sleeping a lot. At any moment in this contact between you and I, I'm not at all clear what you're taking in from me and what you're not. I'm not at all clear what you're asleep to or what you're awake to. There seems to be something that registers with you and then it seems lost, what I call a kind of deadening, as if you can resolve it without really thinking about it, or that you kind of take in but don't really make your own, you don't really assimilate it, you don't really take in."

- "I mean you know the difficulty of having a boyfriend, a relationship—you find it so difficult to meet in an engaged way—and something else, I think what you are doing to me might make you realize, because very much what you've described about your position in your family is that 'I wasn't allowed to exist' … Almost to talk to you, my words might have been interesting but it was as if I really had to struggle to say, 'Look I'm trying to talk to you or even talk with you,' not just because you are elusive but because *I* wasn't allowed to really exist." [Patient is moved, and reaches for a tissue].

Qualities of in-transference interpretation

The current definition of in-transference interpretation is relatively spare, in that its focus is on the therapist's intent to clarify the patient's current feelings or actions in relation to the therapist himself. It may be helpful to consider the examples of in-transference interpretations according to (a) how the interpretations are anchored: (b) to which features of patient–therapist interaction they are directed; and (c) the kind of patient–therapist engagement they appear to foster.

(a) Anchorage The first thing to observe is that in-transference interpretations are anchored in the immediate here-and-now of the patient–therapist exchanges ("There seems to be something that registers with you and then it seems lost"). They tend to be specific to what has just happened or is happening, and although they occasionally make reference to links with other relationships or with recurrent patterns of relating ("in the questionnaire two of the things you mentioned," "you know the difficulty of having a boyfriend, a relationship," "what you've described about your position in your family is"), these instances are immediately followed by reference to current transactions. Therefore in-transference interpretations are essentially local and tightly focussed, rather than general or abstract.

(b) Focus Secondly, in-transference interpretations are focused as follows:

(i) on how the patient experiences the therapist, including qualities of anxiety and defence (e.g., "I don't know the motive for your need to know this but it's clear you need the spotlight on me");

(ii)   on the patient's focus of attention, including what the therapist is think-
       ing or doing ("You see you have to focus on what is in my mind"); and

(iii) on what the patient is trying to *do*. This "doing" is sometimes framed
       in terms of the patient's attempts to deal with his/her own mental states
       ("There seems to be something that registers with you and it then seems
       lost, what I call a kind of deadening," "you kind of take in but don't really
       make your own"), but more often in terms of how the patient is attempting
       to configure the interaction with the therapist ("not just because you are
       elusive but because *I* wasn't allowed to really exist"). Often in-transference
       interpretations refer to how the patient is maneuvering him/herself and
       the therapist to feel certain things or to adopt a prescribed role within the
       exchange ("I'm not at all clear what you're asleep to or what you're awake
       to"). His/her actions in relation to the therapist, whether involving mani-
       fest actions such as what he/she says or mental actions such as projecting
       feelings into the therapist, are often addressed (note: this does *not* mean
       that interpretations about the patient putting feelings into the therapist
       are encouraged). This kind of interpretative work gives emphasis to how
       the patient deals with the therapist's own stance, and, in particular, to the
       ways the patient experiences and uses what the therapist offers by way of
       statements that are intended to express understanding.

(c) Style Thirdly, the style of interpretation is direct, in the sense that the
therapist does not explicitly invite the patient to reflect with him/her on his/
her observations or conjectures, but instead articulates what s/he believes s/
he is witnessing on the basis of evidence that is also available to the patient
(and which therefore can be disputed). Obviously, s/he is also presenting his/
her observations so that the patient can make use of them—and as we have
seen, s/he pays close attention to the patient's reactions. Having said this, in
the excerpts a substantial number of the therapist's interventions began with
"You see ...," or "I think," and this conveys how s/he is putting a viewpoint
that s/he hopes the patient may understand or at least consider.

The above illustrations are intended to highlight features of interpretative
activity that are likely to feature in BPT, but not to prescribe that everything
the therapist says should conform to these characteristics. Much more important is that a therapist engages in sensitive therapeutic work directed to giving
a patient a sense of being understood, while not also experiencing the therapist as needing to deflect from, or as condoning or condemning, what is really
happening. At the core of the therapeutic stance is an effort to confront and
face current emotional reality in the patient–therapist relation, in conjunction
with and for the benefit of the patient.

Finally, it is worth observing that the psychotherapist plays an active role in BPT (Hobson and Kapur 2005 provide evidence of my own high rate of in-transference interpretations when conducting assessment consultations). In BPT, there is urgent work to be done in helping to unfold, identify, and understand those of the patient's relatedness patterns that are a source of ill-health. Although a small number of major relatedness themes will recur again and again in the course of therapy, both in moment-to-moment interactions and over more protracted periods of time, it is vitally important to express understanding of what is happening in the therapeutic relationship as often as the opportunity arises—provided, of course, it is possible to express that understanding in a way that is sensitive to what a patient needs at any moment, and what he or she is able to find helpful.

Here the Manual ends.

Case example revisited

Over the remainder of this book, I shall be teasing out how the principles outlined in the Manual are translated into clinical practice, though, in reality, these principles are distilled from clinical practice. To conclude this chapter, I take a first step by revisiting the very beginning of Ms A's assessment consultation (Chapter 3). My aim is to complement my earlier discussion by indicating how the therapeutic interventions bear the hallmarks of Brief Psychoanalytic Therapy. I should add that when I wrote the following three paragraphs of clinical description, I had not anticipated they would be reviewed in this way, and I have not changed them since.

> Ms A. arrived on time for her assessment consultation. She had a downtrodden look, and tousled fair hair. She asked me where she should start. When I looked at her but did not reply, she said how, if there is no structure in a situation and she does not get feedback, she does not know where to begin. She said that once before she had had a therapist who sat in silence, and it was not very helpful. Perhaps she herself could sit here saying nothing, or she might just talk about things that are not important.
>
> I took up with Ms A how she seemed to trust neither herself nor myself. She might not deal with the most important matters, and I might simply sit in silence, which would be useless. At the same time, I added, she referred to a possible option of becoming silent herself.
>
> Ms A said that she is simply not used to this kind of situation, so unstructured. I said she conveyed a need to have someone either taking the lead, or reacting to what she said. Although her initial stance was to half-dismiss this notion, she soon returned to say how difficult it is if she doesn't get a response.

In this brief commentary, I shall touch upon themes roughly in the order in which they appear in the Manual.

First and foremost, the therapist focuses on the here and now of the transference. Even in the opening moments of the consultation described in this excerpt, I addressed aspects of Ms A's relations with myself that I judged to be happening at that moment. I did so, believing that in all probability, they would include feelings and defences that were characteristic of Ms A. I said how Ms A seemed to trust neither herself nor myself, and remarked that Ms A seemed to anticipate how I might behave and how she might respond. Subsequently, I commented on what she seemed to feel she needed from me.

It can be observed that at this point in our meeting, I did not ask questions, nor did I offer explanation or reassurance. Rather, my interventions represented my best efforts to register the meaning of what Ms A was communicating both verbally and non-verbally, and to articulate some of this in words. I framed my understanding in a way that I hoped would help Ms A to recognize her own stance. I gave thought to whether Ms A was going to be able to hear what I said and how I was saying it, or whether she was too persecuted for this to happen.

Of course, it was open to Ms A to dispute what I said. If this had happened, and if I had felt Ms A was right, or perhaps that my evidence was too provisional, then I would have acknowledged these things. As it happened, Ms A seemed quick to see how I was working hard to understand her. This amounted to one form of integration, because communication between us became more open and honest. At the same time, it seemed to prompt reflection in Ms A's own mind.

There are several rather different observations contained in my description of Ms A's relations with myself. Each of these corresponded with aspects of my own experience of what was happening between us, in the countertransference. Almost from the start, I felt a pressure to behave differently. In particular, Ms A not only appealed for feedback but also made it abundantly clear that a silent therapist was unhelpful. Of course, this had a reasonable component, even though my unresponsiveness to Ms A was more or less limited to when at the outset, she asked me where she should start. There was also a particular coloring to Ms A's remarks. Not only had I to take on board Ms A's anticipation of a silent therapist, but in addition, I sensed my need to avoid the twin dangers of either living out that role, or overcompensating by reassuring Ms A or myself that I do not sit in silence. The form of my response was to express my understanding that responsiveness was a serious matter for her. Ms A confirmed this.

When I referred to Ms A trusting neither herself nor myself, I used the notion of "not trusting" to capture further elements that featured in my countertransference. I felt she experienced a lack of trust in me, but more than this, was actively untrusting toward me.

This exchange may serve to illustrate what it means to promote a move toward integration. At the very moment Ms A was untrusting, a mistrust that would almost certainly have included mistrust about my ability to understand her and respond meaningfully, I remarked on that state of mistrust. This comment, which had been preceded by my working on my own experience of being mistrusted, amounted to a direct challenge to Ms A's active expectation that I would be unreceptive and insensitive. Both current and subsequent evidence suggested that at this moment, I was accurate in my understanding of Ms A *and* responsive in a non-retaliatory way in communicating that understanding to her. I think it took some moments before the impact registered, but then there was movement to a more trusting atmosphere.

Let me return again to the countertransference. When I chose not to respond to Ms A's initial question-cum-plea about where she should start, I felt anxious. Ms A might have felt attacked, or become very angry, or have felt rejected, or whatever. If so, I would have needed to experience (but not necessarily comment on) myself as the source and target of such feelings, and take up these matters in the face of distress and confrontation. And, no doubt, Ms A was not happy with how I was behaving. I felt pressured to follow her script for our respective roles, with me cast as an indulgent and kindly doctor and she as a naïve and dependent patient. However, my anxieties changed as I faced the prospect of being berated and punished. In response to what Ms A felt was an unfulfilled need, namely for me to take the lead and respond sympathetically to her helplessness, she told me that she herself might sit here saying nothing. The defiance in her statement was partly disguised, as was the fear she expressed immediately after, that I might find what she said unimportant. But Ms A's own self-assertive agency had become manifest and available for explicit comment. Once again, a small dose of integration was in prospect. At this point I became more confident about Ms A's resourcefulness.

It remains to consider the quality and style of my interventions. The Manual suggests a therapist should aim to provide understanding when the patient has done something in the therapeutic relationship that is germane to treatment through its emotional significance, not something of which the patient is immediately aware, and something of which the patient can become aware through reflection on what has just happened between patient and therapist. I believe that what I said in this tiny fragment of a consultation more or less conforms to this description. I shall not dwell further on how my remarks were anchored in the here-and-now exchanges between Ms A and myself, nor how their focus was on Ms A's experience of myself and what she was doing to try to maintain her balance. Even though one really needs verbatim transcripts of the kind we shall come to shortly to establish the fact, I think the directness of my style is portrayed accurately. What I said was forthright, but I hope sympathetic. The way I behaved was not tentative nor negotiating, but neither was it dogmatic nor impervious. I trust that what happened subsequently in the consultation and treatment (Chapter 3) bears out these claims.

In Chapter 6 we revisit the manualized principles of Brief Psychoanalytic Therapy from a fresh direction, through verbatim records of patient–therapist dialogue.

Therapeutic dialogues I

Introduction

In this chapter, the focus moves away from stories of patients who enter treatment to the nature of interpersonal transactions within particular sessions of Brief Psychoanalytic Therapy. Instead of drawing on therapists' narratives of events in psychotherapy, I shall represent patient–therapist dialogues through edited transcripts of audiotaped sessions. This means we can follow what therapist and patient actually said to one another, verbatim.

In Chapter 4, I drew on a therapist's notes of what transpired in the final therapeutic session with a patient already introduced through a report of the assessment consultation. In the present chapter, I record verbal exchanges that are abstracted from even this limited amount of context. If we are prepared to forgo information about the background of people in treatment, and relinquish natural inquisitiveness about the history of a given individual's therapeutic engagement over time, then we have little choice but to concentrate on details of the verbal exchanges between patient and therapist. This should set us in a position to examine certain technical aspects of Brief Psychoanalytic Therapy, at a fine-grain level.

Before I come to report clinical material, I want to consider some further implications of dwelling on short sequences of dialogue taken from transcripts of audiotaped sessions.

The data

The investigative strategy adopted here may be anathema to some psychotherapists. How on earth can you think about psychotherapeutic process *except* in the context of knowledge about the patient's past and present relationships, not to mention his or her presenting complaints, anxieties and aspirations, and social context? How can you set aside these sources of meaning about a person, and suppose you are left with enough that is meaningful?

More than this, why sacrifice the depth and richness in psychotherapists' own accounts of their work? Even novice trainee therapists' accounts of sessions communicate so much about intersubjective transactions between patients and themselves. This is not necessarily because the trainees know what they are revealing, but because, whether intentionally or not, they convey how they are caught in the currents of interpersonal feeling and action. Although such material is subjective, it reflects intersubjective transactions that are at the very core of psychodynamic understanding. When a therapist has appropriate training and psychoanalytic ability, then that therapist's account of his or her work, including process notes of what the patient and therapist said to one another and reflections on the therapist's feelings in the countertransference, provide vivid insights into the ways the patient functions.

This is a strong argument. I, too, would prefer to supervise a therapist who brings detailed session notes of the form "the patient said … I said," rather than, for example, watching a videotape or reading a transcript of what transpired. I agree that what might be lost in terms of veridical reporting is more than offset by the gains that accrue from a therapist's particular way of reporting and talking about the therapeutic encounter. But, of course, supervising a clinician's work, or understanding the patient as a whole person, is not the only matter on which one might wish to focus. In order to study other aspects of psychotherapy, different methods are appropriate.

I know from experience that some psychotherapists will feel so disabled by the absence of facts pertaining to a person's emotional life that both metaphorically and literally, they will be inclined to close the book on the present undertaking. I have encountered such incomprehension and skepticism from colleagues before. I recall presenting the study in which Raman Kapur and I were studying how a therapist (myself) gives transference interpretations in assessment consultations (Hobson and Kapur 2005). In pursuit of this aim, we identified and mapped out both the occurrence and content of interpretations in transcripts from videotaped sessions. We were not *for these purposes* considering individual patients as individuals with their own personal stories, nor dwelling on the content of the sessions as a whole. In our paper, we reported how such interpretations proved to be much more frequent than those recorded by other investigators. More importantly, we could illustrate how this made sense, given the quality of my interventions. These were very different to the transference interpretations studied in previous research, and were akin to those that appear in the BPT Manual. However, many psychotherapists in the audience found all this incomprehensible. They could not grasp the rationale for our unfamiliar approach.

From a conventional scientific viewpoint, of course, the problem with a therapist's account of what transpires in a session is that it is selective and to an unmeasureable degree, biased. From this vantage point, the only corrective to bias is to establish that independent raters can agree in their judgments about publicly available representations of what actually happens in a therapy. Anything less is not to be trusted. What we need, these scientists would argue, are videotapes or audiotapes of sessions.

Contrary to what naïve researchers sometimes believe, however, recordings of one kind or another do not provide the definitive form of evidence for emotional transactions in psychotherapy. Much that is most emotionally subtle and personal in face-to-face conversations may elude the camera, especially a camera set at right-angles to the patient–therapist axis. There are also questions about the potentially distorting effects of the recording itself. The intrusion of this third presence in a session, one that gives an unknown audience access to intimate exchanges, surely affects what takes place.

All this is true, but the critical issue is how much is lost and how much gained by any methodological approach. Notwithstanding our reservations, we may ask how much one *can* discover both about individual patients, and about the therapeutic process, through recordings of one kind or another. Personally, I have been surprised how telling details available from recordings sometimes offset restriction in other sources of information about the transference and countertransference, or about a person's history.

At the end of the day, the proof of the pudding is in the eating. We may be optimistic or pessimistic about the yield from the present methodological approach that employs verbatim excerpts from transcripts. Either way, it may be enlightening to discover whether our attitudes change as we review transcripts and see what turns up.

Whatever one's views, transcripts of interviews are essential if one is to document what therapist and patient actually said to one another, in sequence. A therapist's verbal interventions are direct expressions of the therapist's stance and interpretative technique, so they provide invaluable, albeit not exhaustive, evidence of therapeutic activity. Moreover, as we shall come to see in later chapters, they allow independent raters to evaluate qualities of intervention, and thereby provide the basis for scientific exploration.

Meanwhile, it is worth being prepared for something peculiar about the experience of sifting through transcripts. It is natural for readers of clinical descriptions to expect a brisk narrative flow that has coherence and momentum. In laboring over the details of transcripts, whether of everyday conversations or clinical exchanges, one needs to be prepared for hesitations, interruptions and repetitions, and not a few moments of clumsiness. Yet these are what conversations, including conversations between patients and therapists, are like. Although here I have been light with the editorial touch, the excerpts presented here are actually remarkably fluent. But they are selected, and by no means fully representative of any given therapy.

Therapeutic interventions

By and large, therapeutic interventions are not meant to be highly elaborate constructions, nor are they to be delivered with a theatrical flourish. They are carefully considered communications, grounded in evidence that the therapist gleans from what the patient says and does, and from all else that contributes to the transference and countertransference.

Given that the transference is mostly about repeating patterns of relatedness, interpretations of these patterns are likely to need repeating as well. It is frequently the case that a therapist will feel that interpretations for which there is good evidence, and which appear to offer vital insights into a patient's functioning, deserve such repetition with minor variations and perhaps with fresh, explicit anchorage in what has just happened in the session. Often, too, patients have difficulty in taking on board what a therapist says, for a variety of motives and reasons. Therefore in transcripts, we should expect to find therapists returning to themes that are dominant in any phase of a session or treatment.

There are additional features of therapeutic interventions I should like to flag up in advance. Most importantly, therapists are especially attentive to patients' attempts to shape and control communication with themselves. This is not only because such happenings are critical for understanding a patient's personal relationships, especially those that involve dependency, but also because they reflect the patient's characteristic mental actions and inclinations. Indeed, they are important for more than understanding; they are key for advancing the therapeutic process. They give a therapist direct access to what is going on interpersonally, within the session. That access allows the therapist to act on what is happening. If it proves possible to promote a shift in the immediate person-to-person exchange, then intrapsychic change in the patient can follow.

In Brief Psychoanalytic Therapy, the therapist's primary challenge is to feel the transference (largely through the countertransference), see the transference (largely but not exclusively through what the patient says and how he or she says it), and characterize the transference to him or herself. Of course, a therapist will be contemplating how the patient's description of outside relationships or everyday interpersonal events might be *relevant* for the patient's current engagement with the therapist him or herself. But even *if* there were strong concurrent evidence that a mapping on to the session was justified, a therapist might well wait until direct evidence emerged and only then address the current feelings toward the therapist. Once those feelings have been identified and understood, then there is an option of addressing whether the feelings occur in other circumstances.

In this respect, it may be helpful to contrast what a Brief Psychoanalytic therapist tends to do, with what he or she tends not to do. It is very rarely the case that an on-the-ball therapist is inclined to say something like: "You are describing feelings toward your parents/colleagues/friends/rivals/etc., but I wonder if you are having similar feelings toward me in this session." Why? Well, imagine yourself in the place of the patient. At best, you are being invited to do a bit of intellectual-cum-emotional gymnastics, picturing how you might transpose the feelings you have toward a family member, friend, or acquaintance on to the person of the therapist. At worst, a patient may feel the therapist is grasping at straws, and for reasons of theoretical presupposition rather than conviction. This is why I have stressed the directness as well as focus of a therapist's interpretative activity.

The practice of Brief Psychoanaltyic Therapy

I shall interpolate brief comments as the transcripts of this chapter unfold. My principal aim is to make explicit how the clinical material reflects the third therapeutic principle articulated in the BPT Manual, as follows:

> The psychotherapist's task is not only to understand how the patient is experiencing him/herself and the therapeutic setting, but also to determine the patient's role in shaping the interpersonal exchanges within psychotherapy. Often this will entail the psychotherapist recognizing what the patient does to deflect from or otherwise evade conflictual or aversive states of mind.

In fact, much of the material to come also reflects the remaining two principles, namely how a therapist tends to focus on the ways in which a patient relates to the psychotherapist him/herself, and draws on the therapist's own countertransference experience. As it happens, such features of a therapist's stance are not obvious in what follows here, although they are implicit on many occasions when a therapist comments on how a patient is shaping current communication. What is most prominent in these vignettes is how the therapist addresses what the patient does to deflect from intimate contact with the therapist as well as with the patient's own mind.

Each of these two transcripts illustrates something else that is important in Brief Psychoanalytic Therapy. The therapists are concerned to consider the implications of the ending of treatment.

I shall make a final anticipatory remark. The first transcript is rather long, even allowing for the fact that I interpolate two discussion sections. I ask readers to persevere, because the material gathers depth as it unfolds. I shall review some principal themes once the excerpt has concluded. I should add that, as for other session transcripts given in this book, this session was the only one in the treatment that was recorded and transcribed. The patient had been asked about the recording in advance, in fact at the very beginning of treatment, and had given written permission for audiotaping to take place.

The therapeutic dialogues

Transcript 1, part 1

The patient (Pt) who appears in the following transcript of an audiotaped session was a middle-aged woman referred for depression. She was said to have had an aggressive father, and to be someone who adopted the role of supporting other people, including her siblings in childhood, but had difficulty relying and depending on others. In the assessment consultation, it emerged that she was feeling out of control. However, she showed a striking lack of curiosity about the significance of matters that seemed important for her emotional life. She said that addressing her difficulty in establishing close relationships was low on her list of priorities.

Here is a somewhat condensed version of a part of a session toward the end of treatment with a female trainee psychotherapist (T). Earlier in the book (Chapter 2), a section of this transcript was used to illustrate Brief Psychoanalytic Therapy. Given that it captures a late session, the transcript reflects something of the work that has been done thus far. The therapist is commenting on patterns of relatedness with which she is already familiar, as well as capturing the present transactions. We pick up the story after the patient had introduced a theme from the previous session that concerned her difficulty in staying with feelings. She conveyed how she can easily protect herself from others by being condescending and putting them down, as well as prevent the unexpected by clinging to what is familiar and well rehearsed.

T: I think that you do it here, too, you always talk … I was still speaking and you really formulated an answer. Just now as we have spoken, when I was saying that it is difficult for you to stay with the things that you don't know, in the hope of connecting with you and helping you to stay with that, you then say, you then come back with a counter-argument and it is a way of getting away from that confusion, not-knowing, panic.

PT: I agree and I'm not gonna counter-attack or argue. The thing is I feel that I would have too much to lose to just be, to just go with the flow and just show my feelings. The shell that I have is probably very, very thick and it just …

T: You see it's not as if you don't, you're not in touch with feelings or you don't know these feelings, because you tell me about them, but then you move away from it. For example, you tell me there's confusion, you tell me that there are these feelings that you don't like and you don't want to approach them in your mind, you move away from them. You say that the sessions are ending and that there are feelings about that; what then happens is that we don't go deeper, you can't explore them further. You quickly move away to what you know, that is also important but it doesn't allow you to get a different dimension, to experiment with a new way. So you very quickly and subtly go off on to what you know, and that is a loss for you, I think. A loss for you here, and I imagine a loss more broadly in your life.

Reflections on part 1

These exchanges portray how the therapist works hard to pin down the patient's attempts to avoid difficult things in her mind, including confusion and other unpleasant feelings. Among these are feelings about the impending ending of treatment. The therapist attends both to the way the patient behaves, overtly, in their dialogue (e.g., "I was speaking and you really formulated an answer," "then you come back with a counter-argument," "you quickly move away to what you know") and to her reasons for doing so, as well as the psychological implications that ensue ("getting away from that confusion, not-knowing, panic," and "'that is a loss for you, I think"). Those implications apply not only in the session, but involve "a loss more broadly in your life."

The therapist's interpretations are direct, and apply to present goings-on. She describes, up-front and explicitly, what she sees the patient doing, and anchors it in specifics of what has just and is now transpiring. It is clear that the patient recognizes that what she is hearing is not speculation, but an account of how things are. This is no wonder, given the evidence that underpins what the therapist is saying.

Transcript 1, part 2

The excerpt continues as follows:

PT: I agree, regarding the … I've always, the state of mind or frame of mind that I am in now, there is one side that says I wish that I could have longer sessions and another side that says I still have to live my life and what if that person wasn't there. You know I am a grown-up girl and in life you're alone and why are you expecting somebody to try to fix your problems, not that I would know how to fix them 100 per cent. I would probably put a band-aid on it, but life goes on.

T: So there's a part of you that really looks down on the you that has desires, wishes for more sessions, wishes for connections, closeness. Push this aside, you don't need it, you can do it, you're a grown-up girl. It's almost shaming to have this desire.

PT: Maybe more, sorry, maybe they're linked to a weakness, why I identify them as a weakness and also I'm not shaming the other part in the way that … but it's I, it feels like there is a strong part and a weak part and the strong part is trying to sort things out and full of energy and "oh, let's not waste time" and you know, you have felt for a very long time like this, or you kind-of bury those feelings, but hey, you're here and it hasn't killed you and has made you maybe stronger. It defines what you are today, what I am today: somebody with certain issues that I dealt, I have dealt with, not 100%, but I can't say they're sorted because they're not.

It's as if I needed to pick myself up and move on. It's as if I was not lecturing myself but as if there was a little child with a grown-up person in it. The grown-up person was protecting the child by telling her, don't feel like that, you should feel strong, it's you've been hurt, but not everybody is gonna hurt you, you just have to be careful and not really trust people straight away, because trusting them means they're gonna manipulate or abuse you or hurt you but I'm here, protecting you … [P talks about difficulties with her father] … It's the same at work, I've always worked in management and always was the only girl there. I felt that I fitted in because I could compete with those people on that level and that I was way better than them …

Reflections on part 2

Here the therapist takes up further aspects of the patient's attitudes that are expressed both between the patient and others, including the person of the therapist, and between the patient and herself. In particular, the therapist comments how the patient looks down on herself when she has desires and wishes, for example for more sessions or more connectedness with others. The patient herself amplifies how she sees weakness within herself, and idealizes what she sees as a strong part. More than this, she provides rich detail of the process, as a supposedly grown-up figure within herself says "you just have to be careful and not really trust people straight away, because trusting them means they're gonna manipulate or abuse you or hurt you but I'm here, protecting you."

There is an extensive psychoanalytic literature (e.g., Fairbairn 1952; Rosenfeld 1971; Steiner 1993) on such seemingly self-protective, but actually self-depriving, alliances within a person's personality.

Transcript 1, part 3

As the excerpt continues, the therapist takes up what the patient has just said about competing with colleagues:

T: And you connect with others, you have this sort of competition, matching them and remaining ahead in your mind. As you say, you were better than them. But I think it is at the cost of the deeper connecting that I'm talking about. If we keep it here, because this is the situation that we both know best in a way, it's difficult to stay with a, with a wish, with the desire, with a longing—that does remind me of what you said, that's it's only recently you've been able to be more open about your love within your family. There's something really shaming about exposing that needy, wishing side of you and I think very much here with respect to the sessions ending, it is difficult to stay with wanting more, wishing for more, feeling the sadness over what hasn't been achieved.

PT: Everything that you said I agree with; of course I would like more sessions. Because I cannot say that the frame of mind I'm in at the moment is going to be there when I'm uplifted and everything, for a long time.

I think I agree with you that we need to go deeper, and still I'm not doing it. I have changed a little bit, I try to be less judgmental but it feels very unnatural, as if I was biting my tongue. I just want to blurt it out, but I'm not doing it because as I said in former sessions, I want to be appreciated, I want to have like a proper conversation, I want to be able just to relax and not be just waiting to attack, because that is how you make friends.

T: That's when I make a comment that is aimed at feelings, this other side of you kicks in. This side that is winning, is superior, doesn't need anybody, competes with me—and it doesn't let the other side benefit from my thoughts.

PT: Is that how you feel, like I try to compete by not letting you in 100 per cent or by counter-arguing? Because I feel those arguments are valid. That you see me as feeling superior? I don't feel superior.

T: But you said you feel like that in relation to the work situation where you were part of the management with these men, you felt you could match them, in fact you were ahead. I'm talking about something subtle, to do with when there's a chance to connect more deeply, there's also this other side that comes in and wants to stay ahead. I'm not saying you do it consciously, but you do respond very quickly when I say things. Already you've got an answer in your head and this is a way of not allowing the other to get closer to you, because it's this independent side that knows it, knows how to respond, even before the other has given you all there is.

PT: Now that you are saying it, it's like the beginning of a smile coming. I could identify many instances where I haven't let the other person talk. I would only allow them a very … I was always ahead, even with my best friend. Where sometimes he tells me, "Let me finish, because already you …"

I think it's because I've been doing this for such a long time that it's boiling inside of me where I can't hold it back, I can't. How do I get my mind to just absorb everything that they say, and just try not to find a situation or conversation or subject or anything, an example that would either illustrate or conflict with what they say.

T: Just then, I'm sorry to stop you, but just then was a good example. You had started telling me that even you best friend tells you "Let me finish," and then you move on to another level, a more adult level whereby you've understood it all. So what's then taken away from here, from this space, from us, is a kind of Poirot material, my friend tells me this and this is what happens and this is what I feel and this is what he feels. You go on to the explanation, which is, you know, it's useful, but it's keeping things at a particular level.

But you begin, in response to my comment, you say, well this does happen to me, in fact even my best friend says let me finish. Then the kind of nitty gritty of that situation and the emotions disappear, because then you go on to the next level.

PT: I am angry. How do I change that?

T: It is difficult to allow yourself to absorb what I've just said.

Discussion

In many respects, this patient and her therapist are thinking on similar lines. At least in part, this reflects their joint work from previous sessions. So one might ask: what new is the patient discovering in this window of time, and how is the therapist helping her develop her insight and her range of options for shaping her conduct in future?

I think we can see that the therapist makes substantial efforts to show Ms C how some of Ms C's own rather abstract formulations are applicable to the specifics of her present behavior in the session. It appears that this therapist is concerned that Ms C does not remain on an abstract level, but appreciates that what she is describing about her tendencies is in fact happening *now*. Not only is it happening in relation to the therapist, but this fact allows one to trace the serious implications for the patient's mental functioning as well as her capacity to achieve intimacy.

Alongside this, the therapist explores the same or similar phenomena from a variety of perspectives, each of which affords further purchase not only on what is happening, but why. In the opening part of this excerpt, for example, the therapist says, "I was still speaking and you really formulated an answer," and continues by referring this back to the theme initially introduced by Ms C, namely her difficulty of staying with feelings, now re-framed as reflecting ambivalence about sustaining openness toward the therapist. The therapist adds that the motive seems to be Ms C's wish to get away from confusion, not-knowing, and panic.

Ms C herself develops the matter further: she has too much to lose to go with the flow. The therapist is keen to follow up with more precision. It is not that Ms C is unaware, it is that she moves away. Again the therapist anchors this point in something immediate and important that took place shortly before, namely Ms C's having spoken about feelings concerning the forth-coming ending of treatment. The therapist proceeds to lay out the cost in that Ms C forsakes the chance to explore and experiment.

A little too quickly, perhaps, Ms C remarks on her mixed feelings about the ending, and again she provides something more. She describes how she feels she has to manage by herself, one can't depend on others to help, even if her own remedy is a band-aid. The therapist sees the importance of this, and now and in a subsequent moment, highlights two motives (for which she had evidence from other parts of the therapy): firstly, that it is almost shaming to have desires, and there seems to be a part of Ms C that looks down on such openness; and secondly, that Ms C has the impulse to compete and win.

This prompts Ms C to reveal that in her mind to "not waste time" and to dismiss vulnerability is to be strong. Soon after, we hear not only of her hav-ing been hurt, but about the side of her warning of the dangers of trusting people. Among the many implications is Ms C's difficulty in depending on, and receiving things from, other people. In due course, the therapist takes this up in the transference, no doubt drawing on her countertransference, as follows:

> That's when I make a comment that is aimed at feelings, this other side of you kicks in. This side that is winning, is superior, doesn't need anybody, competes with me—and it doesn't let the other side benefit from my thoughts.

This formulation is perhaps a little general, but clearly the therapist is speak-ing about experiences with which both she and the patient are familiar in the therapy. Shortly afterwards the patient develops an emotionally alive connec-tion through the story of a friend who says "Let me finish." Yet once again, Ms C somewhat deadens the impact. So, patiently, the therapist returns to show the specifics of how this happens. She tries to steady Ms C, with "It is difficult to allow yourself to absorb what I've just said."

There might be clinicians who find it obscure, why all this should matter and justify such persevering interpretation. The reason is that the processes with which this patient and therapist are grappling are central to Ms C's difficulties in relationships, which she cannot allow to take, and with her lack of fulfillment in other areas of life. If someone cannot allow dependency, vulnerability, and ordinary human neediness to feature in their emotional repertoire, then, as the therapist expressed it to Ms C, this "is a loss for you I think. A loss for you here, and I imagine a loss more broadly in your life."

The therapist's efforts are bang on target. And by and large, they are focussed on what is present in the transference, what is happening now or in the very recent past, and what is shaping *both* the interpersonal communication of the moment *and* what the patient feels, or is protected from feeling. It should be clear how far this focus on the transference contrasts with the kind of pre-formulated focus that serves as the prime topic for discussion in some other forms of brief therapy.

Transcript 2

Here is a second example of therapeutic engagement involving a different female therapist. In this case, the patient was a young man who tended to hold the floor for extended lengths of time, so the text has needed more drastic editing. However, I have tried to capture what immediately preceded the therapist's interventions, so that mostly one can make sense of what may have prompted her to say what she did.

Again I would forewarn readers that at first, this transcript may seem stuttering and unconvincing. In the early handful of exchanges, admittedly punctuated by gaps in the transcript, the therapist says substantially more than the patient. On reading this initial part of the dialogue, one might come to two quite different conclusions. One view is that the therapist is speculating, and the patient's "I guess" responses indicate that he is skeptical and detached. The other view is that the therapist is sensitive, especially to her countertransference experience, and is articulating what is true, but what the patient is unable to express or perhaps even experience fully. By the end of the excerpt, I hope, readers will (like me) feel in no doubt over which view is correct.

Just before the excerpt, the patient had commented on the presence of the tape recorder: "It's making me laugh for some reason." He went on to talk of work he had done with disabled children.

T: I wonder if your joke toward the recorder is a way of us moving away from what you started off talking about, and that's around your vulnerability. Being aware of vulnerability, seeing it in these disabled youngsters and the fragility which you were talking about being aware of from quite young. About fragility and wanting it to have some distance from you. And you create distance, I think, with the joke toward the recorder as you're in touch with some of your own vulnerability and fragility with me.

PT: Yeah, I guess.

GAP

[The patient talks about his closeness to dogs, and concludes:]

PT: ... The dogs are old, so like I say I relate to them more than anybody, and they've only got, they haven't got long, so it's like it's nice to go down there, but it's always melancholy.

T: I think you're wanting to talk about some of those melancholic feelings, but it's, I think there's something about feeling quite fearful, both because you've got to leave the session after, and how much will you be able to hold yourself together. Your anxiety about losing your mind and your worry about time. I think not only the time today, but the time that we have together, will this work, will it be enough.

PT: Yep. I've been, umm, feeling pretty melancholy generally, but I don't know. I don't know what to focus on or to talk about.

GAP

[The patient talked at length about how he can put on a front at parties, but has a fear of opening up. He also talked about a performer coming up to him and getting him to dance, and then walking on as if nothing had happened.]

PT: ... That was always quite useful when I was on stage, because I manage to cover nervousness, but I think there's something about how I get through everything else.

T: I think you are referring to the cost of the façade that you have. That gives the appearance of ease, and that you can move from one situation to the next in this flexible, adaptable way. But you're saying that actually the cost of it is that little really touches you, moves you in a meaningful way and that there's quite a split. On the one hand wanting I think this time to be moving, to have some impact, to understand more about yourself, but you're also aware of the parts of you that can be much more destructive, as a sort of tongue-in-cheek, the way you can use your humor to move away from meaning. And you end up losing out in that respect. Can I be aware of both aspects, that it's important.

PT: I guess that's why this is potentially so difficult …

GAP

PT: … A bit like the kids last week. You know I wouldn't have chosen to go and hang around with a group of disabled kids for two days, and yet it was, it was brilliant and I came out of it thinking: "Well, maybe I ought to … ," well, I've already said that. I've, I've gone blank, by the way. I'm not dwelling on anything, I'm just …

[Pause]

T: You're being aware of your real struggles with intimacy. It makes you go blank. You were talking about an important relationship, then whether you should do more work with disabled people … and being aware of your struggles with intimacy, you had a reaction to that as to go blank. Shut down.

PT: Yeah maybe, maybe. Yeah. I don't know, I just feel tired I suppose. [Long pause]. Funny, usually I feel like this at the beginning.

T: Perhaps the connection sort of made you more in touch with, umm, I think when you say tiredness I wonder if it's more something that's despairing or sad and …

PT: I'm tired of feeling sad. [Pause]

T: I wonder whether some of that—you say tired of feeling sad—that there's a real question around whether you are acceptable, whether another will want you for who you are, or do you have to put on the façade.

PT: Yeah, whether I'm judging them massively because I've fallen in love with someone, but I don't love myself you know. You've got to love yourself to be loved by somebody, or love yourself to love somebody else, whatever that old gem is, something like that. Maybe I kind of lose respect for people if they love me, 'cos they been suckered in sort of thing. … I kind of think, well, how can anyone love me if I don't sort of know who I am or maybe that's what I said, I don't know. The problem is they keep falling in love with me.

T: I think it does feel hard for you to end knowing that there's something more about your own needs and your own neediness. I think you sort of reverse it and say, well, it's the other people who have fallen in love with you. They then have to cope with the disappointment, but I think there's something about your own struggles as well, being aware of your own need and a wish to push that away.

Discussion

Through her sympathetic understanding, this experienced female therapist plumbs the depths of emotional contact just as far as Mr. D can manage. At the same time, she addresses Mr. D's tendency, evident in the session, to use tongue-in-cheek humor to move away from meaning.

A combination of refined feeling and analytic thinking is evident in almost all of the therapist's interventions. For example, in a single sentence not long into this excerpt, the therapist offers a comment that begins with what she thinks he wants to talk about, his melancholic feelings, then refers to how it may be even more difficult with the forthcoming ending of therapy, and concludes with a more specific notion that he may fear being unable to hold himself together.

The therapist's awareness of the patient's vulnerability in no way undermines her commitment to address the cost of Mr. D's defensiveness. She makes no bones about the destructiveness of his throwaway manner. She respects the patient's own need to be understood in a realistic, not indulgent, manner. She says how it is important for Mr. D that she is aware both of his wish to understand more about himself, and his tendency to return to his façade.

Then in the final part of the transcript, the therapist speaks of Mr. D's struggles with intimacy. Soon after, she translates his self-description of being "tired" into that of being despairing or sad. In response to this, the patient achieves just the kind of intimacy with the therapist that so often eludes him in his life, when he says: "but I don't love myself, you know," and then, even more poignantly, explains that he loses respect for people who love him, because they've been "suckered in."

In my view, this is truly psychoanalytic work. If anyone were to disagree, I would like to know on what grounds. Just because the sessions took place at a frequency of once per week, and extended over a mere 16 weeks? My point is not that the therapy amounted to, nor could be equated with, lengthy psychoanalysis, because of course it did not, and could not. The therapy *was* brief and it *was* psychoanalytic. Psychotherapy gave momentum to a developmental process that required depth of contact and understanding between patient and therapist.

As a matter of fact, this particular therapist had been trained as a psychoanalyst. The therapist's humanness and emotional commitment shine through in the manner as well as content of her communication. All this was essential to her qualities as a psychotherapist. To say as much, is to say something about what may be needed, or to what one should aspire, in becoming a clinician who practices Brief Psychoanalytic Therapy.

Chapter 7

The Adherence Manual

Introduction

This chapter is devoted to laying out an Adherence Manual for Brief Psychoanalytic Therapy. The Treatment Manual characterizes the principles of the therapeutic approach, in as succinct a form as possible, and the Adherence Manual details how those principles are likely to become manifest in the to-and-fro of patient–therapist exchanges. The term "adherence" is employed to convey that, if a given treatment is adhering to the principles of Brief Psychoanalytic Therapy, then this should be reflected in the degree to which a therapist's interventions and orientation conform with the descriptions given in the Adherence Manual. Therefore the Manual crystallizes and operationalizes the principal features of what has gone before, in the form of 17 succinctly expressed descriptors of technique, together with principles and illustrations.

I would suggest a certain way to read the Adherence Manual that follows. Firstly, I advise readers to dip in and out, rather than plough through in one go. I am hoping the Manual will be used to clarify what so far has been obscure, and fill out what has been described only briefly. Hold in mind there is a lot of redundancy here. For instance, a given intervention is likely to exemplify a number of descriptors. This should come as no surprise, given that the descriptors amount to reformulations of a small number of themes considered from slightly different vantage points.

Secondly, the Manual is intended to give pointers to the kinds of clinical features on which a therapist is likely to focus, and the kind of orientation the therapist is likely to adopt. The examples I give of what a therapist has (in fact) said in Brief Psychoanalytic Therapy might be taken as illustrating potentially valuable options when framing therapeutic interventions. The Adherence Manual is *not* a "how to" guide to practice, nor is it prescribing what a therapist *should* do.

At many points throughout this book, I focus on what therapists say, or what a therapist might say, in the course of Brief Psychoanalytic Therapy. As I have already indicated, however, this should not be taken to imply that what the therapist says represents the most important part of the therapist's function. On the contrary, were the therapist merely to say things, without being deeply involved in relation to the patient and committed to understanding their mental engagement, then the therapy would be worse than useless. Very likely, it would be positively harmful. And it is often the case that a therapist *not* saying something is also expressive, for instance of the therapist's thoughtfulness or self-restraint. The crux is that depth of interpersonal understanding, and the adequacy with which a therapist can contain the patient's difficult-to-manage emotional states, is more important than any therapeutic strategy the therapist might employ.

At this juncture, then, the Adherence Manual serves as a fresh point of departure from which to understand Brief Psychoanalytic Therapy, but it is not a port of arrival. It is intended to help readers find for and within themselves a clinical orientation from which to consider their therapeutic work. The items of the Manual should then dissolve into the background.

In Chapter 9, we shall consider how the Adherence Manual may be used for the purposes of research. In a research setting, the items of the Manual serve to characterize elements of the treatment in such a way that independent raters can judge whether transcripts of sessions conform to Brief Psychoanalytic Therapy principles. Whereas for now, I am advocating that one works from the surface features of the Adherence Manual to the depth of what they express, in research one uses the surface features in order to operationalize and identify whether those deeper processes are in play. Given that usually, a research perspective is what motivates the genesis of an Adherence Manual, what follows is framed with this research function in mind. For instance, the text is addressed to someone whose task is to rate a transcript according to the 17 items elaborated in the Adherence Manual.

BPT Adherence Manual

This brief Manual is intended to clarify items on the BPT adherence rating form. It is *not* expected that when filling in the form, raters will need to return to this Manual often, because that would be laborious and interfere with the process of rating.

There are 17 items on the BPT adherence scale, each of which should be rated from 0–4 for the degree to which the item characterizes this therapist's technique in the transcribed session. If the item clearly and accurately captures what the therapist (T) is doing and/or attempting to do in the session, then score 4: if the item describes a form of intervention that is clearly very different from what T is doing and/or attempting to do, then score 0.

Any given therapist intervention or interpretative style may exemplify a *number* of descriptions on the adherence scale. This is reflected in the examples below, many of which could have been used to illustrate several items. The issue is not whether a rater can find separate interventions for each item, but rather, whether therapist technique across a session is characterized by each of the descriptors. Do not worry if you feel the ratings overlap.

The items on the adherence scale are roughly clustered into three subsections for the purposes of this Manual, but there is substantial overlap. The groupings are introduced to help raters orientate to the material, that is all. And remember: when it comes to rating, the Manual is for backup guidance only. The rating sheet (which lists the items succinctly, as indicated by **bold type** below) should provide much of what is needed.

In what follows, "examples" are supposed to exemplify the items, sometimes through imagined therapist statements; "illustrative therapist interventions" are more or less verbatim examples from transcripts. In fact, I have replaced a handful of the illustrative interventions from the original Adherence Manual (which of course did not contain examples from the transcripts under study) with what I consider more appropriate exemplars drawn from elsewhere in this book.

Focus on patient–therapist relatedness

1. T tracks specific patterns of *interpersonal interaction and/or relation* between the patient and T

Principle

The point here is that T devotes attention to the pattern of *what the patient feels, says and does in relation to T*. What the patient says or does shapes what is felt or not-felt (or thought-about or not-thought-about) within the relationship. So, too, what the patient feels toward T shapes the patient's thoughts and responses. These qualities of relation are *the* prime focus for T.

Examples

- T might refer to the patient's attitudes experienced and/or expressed toward T (humiliation, contempt, denigration, dismissiveness, concern, and so on).

- T might comment on the position the patient experiences him/herself to be in, such as needing to be polite, or to hide what he/she really feels, or to convince T that he/she is suitable for treatment.

- T will often take up a patient's *response to what T says*, as an especially illuminating manifestation of the quality of the interaction (and such an intervention would also illustrate how T tends to focus on the patient's response to what just happened in the session: see item 9 below).

Illustrative therapist interventions

- "when I make a comment that is aimed at a feeling [you have], this other side of you kicks in—winning, superior, doesn't need anybody, competing with me and it doesn't let the other side benefit from my thoughts." (Here T takes up the patient's response to T's own utterances, and illuminates what happens to the relation between T and the patient.)

- "You see what I'm trying to get back to is, is your way of talking which might be relevant, maybe interesting, but it is really like you said about the last few weeks, keeping you on a certain plane." (T is highlighting that the relation between the patient and T *seems* to be significant, but this belies how it is on a certain plane and in fact avoiding deeper engagement and stultifying progress.)

2. T focuses upon role relationships the patient is attempting to establish or avoid in the session

Principle

T focuses upon ways in which the patient is shaping the current exchanges in order to make sure the interaction is manageable, while less manageable feelings are avoided.

Examples

- T may take up how the patient establishes roles for T and/or the patient. Examples might be: "You stress that I am the expert," or "You want me to be the one who asks questions, which you answer."

- T might note the patient's state or stance toward T. For example: "You step back and observe what I am doing, and it amuses you," or "You are ready to fight back if I say anything you feel is not justified."

- T may comment how the patient requires that T takes such-and-such a view of the patient. Examples might be: "You stress how this is the first time you have come, so you can't be expected to know what to say," or "You make it clear to me how you are going to think for yourself."

Illustrative therapist interpretations

- "You come back with a counter argument and it is a way of getting away from that confusion, not knowing, panic." (T points out that the patient is trying to establish a role relationship in which patient and therapist argue, and refers to the motive of avoiding an unmanageable state of confusion and panic.)

- "There's a sense that I'm encouraging you to do something that feels too much or dangerous and I'm going to drop you, leave you." (T focuses on the threatening role relationship of dependency which needs to be avoided, while at the same time highlighting how this influences the patient's experience of T's interventions.)

3. T addresses the ways in which the patient avoids, controls, or otherwise constrains intimate engagement with T

Principle

T is picking up the strategic maneuvers deployed by the patient to defend him/herself from the dangers (whatever they might be) of intimate and vulnerable interactions.

Special attention may be given to how a patient deals with feelings stirred by separations and—importantly—the ending of this intimate and significant relationship.

Examples

- T might pick up how the patient gives common-sense explanations for what he/she feels, explaining away rather than really getting to grips with difficult issues; or T might note how the patient transforms the personal expression of some event into an objective recounting as if from a third-person position.

- T might point out that the patient is dismissive of anything that could stir conflict or anxiety such as a difficult childhood ("My childhood was just normal, really"), or show how the patient imposes rather limited and stereotyped forms of relatedness ("I need you to tell me/be nice to me, Doctor").

- T might indicate compulsive self-reliance and avoidance of ambivalence stirred by the ending of the therapy.

Illustrative therapist interpretations

- "There's something really shaming about exposing that needy wishing side of you, and I think very much here with respect to the sessions ending …" (implying that the patient is avoiding vulnerability and dependence).

- "in terms of your coming here we have to see that it actually lifts you out of the domain of getting to things that are more personal and sometimes difficult" (implying that this way of coping deflects from potentially distressing states).

4. T highlights what the patient conveys to T about the patient's emotional state in the here-and-now of the session

Principle

It is often important that T picks up, and is explicit about, what a patient is communicating about his/her position and feelings in relation to T. There are two aspects to this. One is that T indicates how T takes seriously *that* the patient is trying to communicate something (although this is not always made explicit). The other is that T is concerned with *what* the patient is conveying. Sometimes the patient has been explicit about this, while at other times T interprets what T considers is conveyed between the lines, or even what is communicated unconsciously.

Examples

- T might reflect how the patient stresses how helpless and pessimistic she feels.
- T might comment how the patient half-conceals irritation that T does not immediately answer her legitimate questions.
- T might take up how the patient feels trapped within a power relation where the patient's own views can be dismissed.

Illustrative therapist interpretations

- "You do your best efforts and then you feel I find fault, when I say that's not good enough and you think ... whatever I do is never any good." (T captures both what the patient experiences in the relation, and the patient's efforts to deal with this.)
- "What you convey is that there is something in you that requires nothing less than perfection." (T takes up what it is like to be the patient, including being in intimidating/intimidated states that were also being experienced—in fact, by the therapist as well as the patient—at times in the session.)

5. T comments on how the patient experiences T's attitudes, thoughts, feelings, and actions concerning the patient and what the patient says, does and feels

Principle

This is a specific aspect of T's focus on current patterns of relatedness toward himself/herself. T may comment on what the patient imagines, thinks, feels, fears, hopes for, or tries to induce in T by way of T's own attitudes toward the patient.

Examples

- T might comment on a patient's anxiety lest T is simply out to impose T's own view
- T might reflect that the patient feels T is out to exploit the relationship for T's own ends
- T might state that a patient feels T will not properly register a patient's vulnerability or need to assert him/herself, or, by contrast, T might remark that the patient feels T *is* able to listen.

Illustrative therapist interpretations

- "as you leave and then what you do in thinking about it is 'oh gosh, oh gosh, he thinks this, he thinks that,' and … you think I'm actually kind of disapproving." (T takes up not only how T is experienced as disapproving, but also how the patient becomes preoccupied and unsettled.)

- "You see how much you have to focus on what is in my mind … what I'm expecting, what I'm thinking, what I'm inquisitive about." (Here T reflects not just on how the patient experiences T, but the patient's whole orientation.)

6. T takes up what the patient is needing T to take account of, and/or hold for/withstand from the patient e.g., anxiety, anger, vulnerability

Principle

T is likely to be explicit about the role and stance that a patient needs T to adopt. T might include specific mention of what the patient wants T to register and grasp about the patient's position, whether in relation to vulnerabilities or strengths and abilities.

T is very aware that patients distribute anxieties or other mental states to other people, so that T might need to experience things for the patient. T is also aware that it is sometimes of value to clarify when this is the case. For instance, T might remark on how a patient has to give T responsibility for taking the lead over the subject matter of exchanges; or T might take up how important it is that T is able to respond to the patient's urgent expressions of need (or anger) without being overwhelmed. However, this item does not necessarily mean that T interprets the patient's need directly—this might be premature and persecutory for some patients—and T might merely convey what seems to characterize T's side of the emotional transaction within a current phase of the session.

T may also make direct or indirect allusion to the emotional importance of T being able to listen to, understand and contain the patient, if necessary with firmness. In other words, either implicitly or explicitly, T is alert to the patient's sensitivity toward T's ability to manage what T him/herself may experience in the course of the interaction.

Examples

- T might state that patient needs T to realize that he/she is not only vulnerable, but also able and quick to make his/her own judgements.

- T might say that that a patient needs both T and the patient to be aware that the patient can be less than honest; or that the patient needs T to be able to sift the trustworthy from the shifty.

- T might express the view that a patient needs *T* to know what it is like to feel anxious and untrusting (in relation to the patient him/herself).

Illustrative therapist interpretations

- "I can see you really are trying today to talk to me. I can, you know, there's a feeling of urgency coming from you even, but I do think it's difficult for you to believe perhaps that you can get something from somebody else." (T feels the patient needs T to take account of the patient's genuine attempt to communicate, and also the patient's pessimism about what can be achieved.)

- "On the one hand wanting I think this time to be moving, to have some impact, to understand more about yourself, but you're also aware of the parts of you that can be much more destructive, as a sort of tongue-in-cheek, the way you can use your humor to move away from meaning. And you end up losing out in that respect. Can I be aware of both aspects, that it's important?" (T indicates not only that the patient has different sides to his personality, but also that he needs T to be aware of how these are contributing to the present communication with herself.)

Specifics of therapist technique

7. T rarely asks questions—and is likely to defer from answering questions immediately—and instead comments on what the patient is doing or feeling or communicating in relation to T. T tends to do this by pointing out rather than asking questions or offering explanations.

Principle

It is not that T is supposed to avoid questions or reference to background conditions that may help the therapist and/or the patient to understand current patterns of relatedness. Rather, a major portion of T's interventions are to make explicit what is happening in the present. T is also concerned to illuminate why this is happening in the present, for instance to protect the patient from certain anxieties.

So, too, when asked a question or challenged directly, T may not-answer the question or not-respond to the challenge directly. The reason is that T wants to understand what is behind the question or challenge. Therefore T may wait, or address what the question seem to convey about the patient's need to find out something (where what the patient may be trying to assess is something about T's stance).

The focus is on what the patient seems to be doing to shape the relationship in conveying what he/she says, or avoids saying or otherwise communicating.

I emphasize, it is not that T avoids asking or answering questions *tout court*. For example, T may return to a question and answer it directly at a later point in the session (T may even say that this will happen, because clearly it is important to respect a patient's right to ask things.) The point is that T's primary concern is to evaluate what it means that the patient is asking this question at this point in the session—and more precisely, what the patient is trying to do and establish *through* asking the question. Similarly, the reason that T mostly avoids asking questions, is that questions elicit answers. Often the patient's emotional response the question is lost, and T is drawn into setting the agenda.

Examples

- T might comment that the patient is becoming excited in asking a question that puts T on the spot; or T might reflect on the patient needing T to withstand uncertainty and discomfort.

- T might observe how the patient has not mentioned the patient's father when talking of childhood, rather than asking about him directly.

- T might suggest that the patient is seeking reassurance by prompting T to reveal things about T, and having the patient's own right to know respected; or T might comment that the patient needs to bring the focus on to T, to create a more manageable interaction.

Illustrative therapist interpretations

- "You try hard to present something interesting and to get things going again." (T points out what the patient is doing, both at the surface level and beneath this, when the patient feels he/she needs to sustain the exchange.)

- "There seems to be something that registers with you and then it seems lost, what I call a kind of deadening, as if you can resolve it without really thinking about it." (T addresses a mental act in which the patient deadens awareness in order to avoid the pain of thinking. The focus is on something of which the patient is probably unaware, but may be able to grasp, as it happens.)

8. T tends to pick up on what the patient has just said, done, or expressed

Principle

It is not important or appropriate to pick up on what has just happened at all moments of a consultation, of course. Remarks that integrate broader features of the patient's relationships, including those outside treatment or in the past, may be apposite. However, this item is intended to highlight a feature that is likely to be prominent at some points in the session, because it reflects how T is addressing qualities in moment-to-moment communicative events.

Examples

- T might note that T has tried to say something, and the patient has interrupted and/or talked on as if T hadn't said anything; or T might suggest how the patient seemed to react to T's looking at his watch, by appearing to not notice.

- T might focus upon what the patient had just said, even though the patient swiftly changed topic.

- T might remark on how the patient felt T's lack of answering a question was an indication of T trying to assert superiority.

Illustrative therapist interpretations

- "Immediately you focus on what I may have read ..." (T illustrates the patient's defensive action in referring to the questionnaire, almost as soon as an initial consultation has begun.)
- "You actually did say to me something like, 'How can I tell you how it affects me?', and I thought that there was something very genuine in that, a real appeal to me you didn't know ..." (T takes up an event that has just passed, to mark its genuineness—this being in contrast to other things that are happening.)

9. When indicated, T makes explicit evidence *in the session and therapy* for statements he/she might make about the patient's state or behavior

Principle

T is working from the surface to depth—or rather, finding depth *in* surface behavior. T focuses on what is identifiable in the current transactions. T is concerned with patterns of interaction which are not only objectively present (i.e., in principle, something that independent clinicians would recognize), but also available for the patient to register and comprehend.

Of course, the patient may not accept that such behavior has meaning, but T is trying to point toward significance by highlighting what the patient is already in a position to notice when this is pointed out.

Examples

- T might say: "When I took up what you were saying in so many words, you ignored my comment and treated what I said as irrelevant," or "Once again you shrug. I don't think you want to register any new idea from me."
- Referring to an autobiographical account that the patient has just delivered, T might observe: "You seem to have been talking to me as if from a third-person stance."
- As already illustrated, T might take up the here and now by comments such as: "When I said you find this difficult, you turned away and seemed to feel it was a criticism of you," or "Just now, when you sat back, I think you'd felt I was listening to you," and so on.

Illustrative therapist interpretations

- "I think a few moments ago you sort of saw ..." (T gives specific illustration of the patient's difficulty in holding on to insight.)
- "the five minutes at the start when we were talking ..." (Again, the point T is about to make is anchored in a specific incident on which T could elaborate if needed.)

10. T comments upon manifestations of development or change in the patient's state and relatedness from moment to moment in the session, and perhaps over longer periods

Principle

This is another manifestation of the closeness with which T monitors the shifting modes of relatedness between the patient and him/herself. The patient is shaping the interpersonal transactions one way, then shifts to another, then another, perhaps in relation to what T has just said.

Examples

• T might note how the patient is in one state of mind for half a minute/session/treatment—for example, controlling and somewhat persecuted—then shifts to another when thinking frees up and something more mutual is allowed to happen.

• T might remark on the patient's change to suspiciousness and mistrust when T has commented on (say) the patient's sensitivity to being mis-treated.

• T may comment on the patient's disappointment/hopelessness when not fully understood.

Illustrative therapist interpretations

• "I think a few moments ago you saw how serious things were, but I think through some process you end up in a position where you sort of lose contact with that." (T tracks a significant change in the patient's awareness.)

• 'I said that you could say, and then what happened was that you went off on a knight's move." (Here the knight's move is an abrupt alteration in the patient's train of thought, to effect a dislocation from unwanted feelings.)

11. T comments upon defensive maneuvers and/or attitudes occurring within the patient's mind that correspond with (and shape) maneuvers manifest in patient–T relatedness

Principle

Often, ways in which a patient experiences and/or attempts to shape the patient–T interaction correspond with experiences and defensive maneuvers within the patient's own mind. This was illustrated in the last two therapist interpretations cited above (for item 10). T is likely to comment upon the implications of such interpersonal *and* intrapsychic processes for the patient's own experiences and capacities of mind. In other words, T might refer to effects within the patient's mental life, not just within the patient–T transactions. From a complementary viewpoint, T's comments on shifts within the session also illustrate, either implicitly or explicitly, the effects of the patient's mental processes and actions.

Examples

- T might note how the patient maintains his/her equilibrium by translating emotional problems into concrete issues such as physical problems, limiting what the patient as well as T can access or address.
- T may note how the patient adopts a dismissive and superior stance both toward T and toward toward parts of themselves or states of mind such as vulnerability.
- T may note how the patient deadens the emotional significance of what happens, so thinking is evaded.

Illustrative therapist interpretations

- "it is difficult to stay with a feeling of wanting more, wishing for more, and sadness over what hasn't been achieved." (T refers to a difficulty that is manifest in the session, but also broadly applicable to what goes on in the patient's mind.)
- "You cling on to the familiar, well rehearsed ..." (Again, this is a statement about the patient's habitual mental stance, exemplified in the current patient–T interaction.)

12. T refers (directly or indirectly) to the significance of the patient taking or avoiding responsibility for his/her own thoughts, beliefs, choices, etc., especially within the session

Principle

This is not meant to convey that T tells a patient to "buck up and behave." Rather, T picks up and may focus upon episodes in which a patient appears to commit himself on the one hand, or evade states of mind on the other.

Examples

- T might note how when the patient says things, it is unclear whether or not the patient actually believes or is committed to what he/she is saying; or T might remark how the patient attributes to T any views or opinions that emerge, rather than thinking for him/herself.
- T might pick up how the patient short-circuits and/or avoids the acknowledgment of difficult feelings.
- T might speak of how the patient turns moments of potential suffering into masochistic churning over, or how he/she makes pain an object of laughter.

Illustrative therapist interpretations

- "You see I don't think you take seriously enough the issue with your panics." (This might seem paradoxical, when the patient was complaining of her panics. What T indicates is that the patient hands over the challenge to think about when, why and how she panics—and the significance of these feelings.)

- "You kind of take in but don't really make your own, you don't really assimilate it, you don't really take in." (T confronts how what seems to be happening, namely the patient listening to what T is saying, is questionable—and raises the possibility that the patient is not committing herself to either agreeing or disagreeing with what is said.)

Overarching features of therapist stance

13. Overall, T's primary concern is to explore the nature of the patient's states of mind and patterns of relatedness toward T, and reveal the significance for the patient's everyday life (rather than to make interpretations about links with the past, although these may occur)

Principle

There are two reasons for this being T's primary concern. If these reasons are understood, this may help to rate what T is doing when he/she *does* link the present with the past or with outside life.

Firstly, T believes that a critical therapeutic factor is T's ability to help a patient re-integrate states of mind that the patient finds difficult to own and to bear. Often, this will involve T making explicit what the patient is finding it difficult to manage and/or is avoiding.

Secondly, T is concerned that conversations over the past or outside life may become defensive, even collusive, retreats from more immediate and important emotional difficulties both within the patient and between the patient and T. Therefore when these *are* discussed—and such discussion can be very valuable—this needs to occur when such discussion does not amount to a (possibly collusive) bid to escape from something else.

Of course a patient needs to talk at length about his/her relationships. T may need to clarify aspects of this. Yet it is to be expected that relatively soon, what is being *talked about* will become relevant in *some* way for understanding the lived, present relationship with the therapist. Then the focus is likely to shift.

It is critical that a major aim of the therapy is to enable a patient to tolerate, rather than avoid, difficult and painful states of mind.

Examples

- T may highlight how difficult it is for the patient to stay with a given feeling or anxiety, without getting rid of it, and may point to an example outside as well as inside therapy.

- T might stress the effects of the patient's ways of controlling what happens both in relation to T, and within the patient's own mind more generally.

- T may observe how the patient appears to feel more comfortable talking about the past or work, than addressing how he/she feels now.

Illustrative therapist interpretations

- "You're again going to the familiar ground of what you know, moving away from your insight, today the insight that it is difficult for you to admit that there are things that you don't know, that there are things you can't do." (T addresses a recurrent theme: not only is T saying something about the present interaction—essentially, pinpointing the patient's inclination to move away from important issues, and avoid awareness of any dependence on T—but also highlighting a general difficulty for the patient in acknowledging he cannot do everything that others can do, and might need others.)

- "So you very quickly and subtly go off on to what you know, and that is a loss for you I think. A loss for you here, and I imagine a loss more broadly in your life." (T points out the broader significance of the patient's interpersonal/intrapsychic moves.)

14. T addresses not only the negative/destructive side of the patient, but also the patient's wish and/or potential ability to make contact

Principle

This is a particular part of T's endeavor to register and recognize what is truly happening, or indeed truly a part of a patient's personality or mode of functioning.

Examples

- T might point out when a patient is controlling or attacking or dissembling (whether in relation to T or the patient him/herself), but also note a patient's capacities to listen, or to think, or to show some response to what T has said, whether that response is positive or negative.

- T might stress how the patient's seeming defensiveness or evasiveness are also communications to T, how difficult it is for the patient to deal with certain conflicts or anxieties.

- T might note how a patient's wish to communicate or share is attacked by something else within the patient.

Illustrative therapist interpretations

- "I think at the beginning of this session you were trying hard, genuinely …" (T stresses the patient's attempts to achieve authentic communication.)
- "well just look at yourself now, this hasn't come without it being built on something, so you must have held on to something." (T tries to consolidate a moment when the patient has made progress, and highlights what this says about the patient's contribution and potential.)

15. T expresses responsibility for what T thinks, says, does, as well as for what T does not know, gets wrong, or overlooks

Principle

It is sometimes thought that in psychoanalytic psychotherapy, T acts omnipotently and omnisciently. Yet, however directly T expresses a view on what is going on, this is clearly (and if necessary explicitly) T's view on the basis of evidence, much of which T can cite. T can revise this view and convey recognition of having been wrong.

However, this is not the same as the notion that T offers tentative hypotheses, because often T has more conviction than this. So, too, T is direct and open about issues for which T is responsible that affect the patient.

Examples

- T might stress how T puts the patient in a position of experiencing the difficulties raised by breaks in, or limitations of, treatment.
- T might acknowledge that, for example, he/she had missed the point of what a patient had been saying, or had collected the patient slightly after the time of the appointment, or had looked at his/her watch to check the time.
- T might also state (often using the word "I") that it is T's view or T's doubt that such-and-such is the case.

Illustrative therapist interpretations

- "I'm not sure if I follow how you're thinking about it." (T makes it clear that T is not omniscient, and is uncertain.)
- "a long gap that's my fault. So it's more than just the mechanics, but somebody actually has responsibility for this and you might have feelings about that." (T takes responsibility for being away, and notes how this has implications.)

16. T conveys, directly or indirectly, that T's major concern is with the truth of what is happening, especially in the session, and does not advise nor condone nor condemn

Principle

In all kinds of ways, T communicates a commitment to facing the truth of what is happening in the session. Even here, if T feels that a patient is not committed to the truth, T's attitude should be firm about the fact that this is happening, and about its implications, rather than condemning. Of course, the truth is many-layered, so T might focus on any number of facts.

Examples

- T might explore whether or not something claimed by a patient (e.g., the patient's lack of insight, or timidity) is actually the case, as illustrated by events in the session.

- T might indicate how the patient attempts to establish a situation that *seems* to be one thing, but in fact is otherwise (e.g., where the patient seems to be thoughtful, but is in fact simply compliant and avoiding any disagreement; or where a patient's confidence belies underlying anxieties).

- T may convey the importance he/she attaches to evidence in the session for what is true—and how interpretation of the evidence may be negotiable, but there is an underlying truth to be uncovered.

Illustrative therapist interpretations

- "'I don't know if you're really yet on board to tackle this." (T emphasizes his/her genuine uncertainty about what is clearly, for T, a serious matter).

- "Yes, it's visible, I can actually see it. Yes, I can see when you shift." (T is confirming the patient's own acknowledgment of a fact, namely that she shifts among different states of mind.)

17. T's manner conveys that *everything matters*. T's predominant attitude is of taking things seriously, especially things the patient is inclined to shrug off

Principle

Everything the patient says and does is treated as potentially significant. T will not presume quite *how* something matters—for instance, lateness can be an expression of self-assertiveness and/or lack of over-zealous conformity, just as it can be undermining—but takes the stance that things are meaningful and worthy of serious consideration. Often this is especially the case when a patient tries to minimize an event's significance.

Examples

- T might take up the potential meanings in Freudian slips or mistakes over recalling the times that had been arranged for sessions.

- T might focus upon a patient's dreams, and what these signify.

- T might interpret a patient's lapses in concentration or focus, or seemingly random associations or non sequiturs.

Illustrative therapist interpretations

- "but I'm serious because we have ... I'm not lecturing you, I'm trying to make you see something." (T illustrates a commitment to taking something seriously that the patient seems to be shrugging off.)

- "You see I think this goes very deep." (T not only marks something that the patient mentions almost in passing, but also stresses how very significant it is.)

The Adherence Manual ends here.

Discussion

It might seem unnecessary and disrespectful to the nature of psychotherapy to have broken down a coherent therapeutic attitude and process in this way. Even if elements of psychotherapy can be characterized and identified, there is a danger that to pursue this approach is to sap the meaning from what is being described. I trust readers will treat this possibility as one open to examination in the light of practice. In the meantime, I fully accept that what has been rendered piecemeal needs to be re-integrated if the nature of Brief Psychoanalytic Therapy is to be recognized for what it is.

Perhaps for the moment, the best way to absorb this chapter might be to forget it. If it has served its purpose, it should have made sense of what might otherwise have remained too abstract. My aim in laying out the Adherence Manual at this point in the book has been to give familiarity to what may have seemed alien or abstruse. But as I have emphasized before, what really matters is a therapist's understanding of, and attitude toward, the patient. The items of the Adherence Manual certainly speak to this, but only in a partial and stilted manner. In Chapter 8, we shall begin the return journey to the whole patient by considering brief clinical exchanges, recorded verbatim, that provide a meaningful context for a therapist's utterances. Rather than working from Adherence items to illustrative interventions, as in the Adherence Manual, I shall give excerpts of transcripts and see how the therapist's attitude and activity exemplify the items. Then in Chapter 9, I shall illustrate how the Adherence Manual functions as a research tool.

Chapter 8

Therapeutic dialogues II

Introduction

The purpose of this chapter is to reflect upon clinical material in the form of extended vignettes that have been transcribed almost verbatim from transcripts of audiotaped sessions involving five different clinicians and their respective patients. Already in Chapter 6, we began to explore how therapeutic principles embodied in the Treatment Manual find expression in a therapist's verbal interventions. Here we take this exploration a step further, and analyze sequences of patient–therapist dialogue according to the technical principles embodied in the Adherence Manual of Chapter 7. At the risk of becoming clunky, I shall point out how given parts of the text accord with items from the Adherence Manual (henceforth labelled as "Item ..." and numbered as in the Manual).

Once again, there is a cost attached to breaking down psychotherapy into fragments that comprise decontextualized patient–therapist exchanges. Although I have chosen to group excerpts of dialogue from each treatment in turn, rather than completely dispersing and mixing up different therapists' interventions, I shall say very little about the patients and therapists involved. One reason (again) is to maintain the anonymity of the individuals concerned. Another is that, providing we take it on trust that when a therapist raises unfamiliar issues into the therapeutic dialogue, these are derived from broader and deeper knowledge of the patient, we really do not need to know more. The exception to this is that often the therapist's countertransference, which of course makes an important contribution to both the manner and content of the therapist's input, has developed over periods of time that extend beyond the brief moments of the exchanges documented. In such cases, I provide a short introduction.

I shall give headings according to numbered "psychotherapies." The reason I do so is that we are concerned not so much with patients or cases, but with transactions within therapeutic engagements. Each of the five psychotherapies described in the chapter was conducted by a different therapist. This matters, insofar as we are considering a type of therapy that should be common to a set of therapists, not simply the therapeutic style of one or two individuals.

In each instance, the excerpts are from a single session, and I shall indicate when there are gaps, that is, when I have edited out some of the dialogue.

Excerpt from first psychotherapy

The following brief span of dialogue comes from the transcript of a session involving a female therapist and a young woman who, just before the excerpt, had spoken of how she does not like herself, and how she's just avoiding everything.

T (THERAPIST): I wonder whether this sounding annoyed and fed up with yourself might be a sort of equivalent to what you were saying about a kind of mindless, almost destructive pastime, and you could really get into having a go at yourself.

PT (PATIENT): Yeah, I could get really into having a go at myself, but then if I wasn't too much having a go at myself, I would turn to the mindless pursuit. Then there's no more having a go at myself. [Note: I have adjusted what I think was a typographic error, changing "wouldn't" to "would."]

T: But I mean right now in here.

PT: Yeah, yeah. Do you know what, I think I'm done. I've wasted the time already.

T: That in itself might turn into it.

PT: Yeah.

T: Having a go and criticizing. When I think recently, it's about the precious time, and your real awareness of there not being a lot of time, we only have today and next week before the break, but I wonder whether something of what we are seeing is that there is so much in your mind and so much that you are feeling overwhelmed by, that it's very difficult to allow yourself to get into it and make that contact with me.

PT: Mmm. That's completely possible. Highly probable.

Discussion

This excerpt is terse and, at first reading, a bit difficult to follow, but I begin with it for the reason that it captures so much of what is essential to Brief Psychoanalytic Therapy.

Firstly, I offer some clarification. I take it that when the patient makes the comment, "but then if I wasn't too much having a go at myself, I would turn to the mindless pursuit. Then there's no more having a go at myself," she is saying that she can alternate between having a go at herself, itself a kind of mindless pursuit, and other forms of distraction with which she is more familiar. Then subsequently, when she says, "Do you know what, I think I'm done. I've wasted the time already," I take it that she is mostly talking about the time already spent in the session, although almost certainly what she says has broader meaning in relation to the patient's life as a whole.

When the therapist comments, "That in itself might turn into it," she is (as she explains subsequently) referring to the patient's own stance with "I've wasted the time already." Her point is that although this latter statement is both true and insightful, it could be twisted to become further grist for the mill of unproductive "having a go and criticizing."

So what takes place in this minute or two of patient–therapist interaction? The excerpt opens with the therapist commenting on what has just been happening in the session, with "I wonder … ," and later she uses the expressions "I mean … ," "When I think," and "I wonder" once again. In this way, she is taking responsibility for her own perspective (Item 15). Yet at the same time as she leaves matters open for further discussion and dispute, given that "I think" is very different from "I know," the therapist is also direct in what she ascribes to the patient. Note she says more than that the patient is self-critical; she remarks that "you could really get into having a go at yourself," indicating that the patient is not only responsible for this mental activity, but also that it becomes rewarding for her. Really getting into something is more than just being defensive.

Moreover, the therapist is acutely aware of the dangers of the patient, and probably the therapist herself, lapsing into generalizations that lack immediacy and lend themselves to seeming insight but amount to avoiding everything. She responds to the patient's reflection that "Then there's no more having a go at myself" by anchoring her view of the activity in the immediate present: "But I mean right now in here." She more or less repeats the message when she comments that the patient's response about what she (the patient) has done already (in the past of the session, and by implication her life) is perhaps a current instance of the same thing. Emotional transactions in the here and very much now are what matter most (Item 4).

It is important that what might be construed as the therapist persecuting/ pursuing/blaming the patient is in fact something very different. At least there is solid evidence that it is something different. The evidence comes not only from other parts of the transcript, but also from the quality of the therapist's tone and the nature of the patient's responses within the present phase of the session. It happens that the excerpt includes the therapist's sympathetic remark that "there is so much in your mind and so much you are feeling overwhelmed by, that it's very difficult to allow yourself to get into and make that contact with me." I think strongly implied although not made explicit at this point, is that the therapist is (Manual Item 6) "taking up what the patient needs the therapist to take account of and/or 'hold' for/withstand from the patient."

Of course, the patient might have experienced the therapist's earlier remarks as persecuting. Does this mean they should have been avoided? How much of value is lost when a psychotherapist, either from fear of seeming (if not being) nasty or insensitive, or out of concern that the patient does not suffer or retaliate, avoids plain talking about the truth of what is happening? Patients can feel relieved when they discover a therapist has the courage to call a spade a spade, and is able to distinguish what is healthy and genuine from what needs to be questioned and challenged. If a patient were to experience persecution, then of course these feelings would need to be addressed. But a therapist who is not prepared to take risks is likely not only to miss vital opportunities to help the patient, but also to convey that the therapist is unable to manage what the patient desperately needs help in managing.

In her final remarks, the therapist refers to what is going on in the patient's mind now, as this influences what is happening in the session. She acknowledges the fine line between what the patient is responsible for, and what the patient feels is out of control and overwhelming. The therapist frames what she says in relation to something she clearly feels is central, namely "that contact *with me*."

Excerpt from second psychotherapy

This session was almost entirely focused on how the female patient managed a difficult negotiation with her female psychotherapist. A fortnight previously, the patient had phoned to say she had had an important workshop to attend and would need to miss a session. Subsequently she failed to attend a further session because she had been "knocked out by nausea ... but I just thought it would be very understandable by you."

In the session that followed, T commented that the patient was trying to maintain a good atmosphere ...

T: ... because in fact you called and asked if the session could be rearranged. I didn't respond to that and I wonder, that doesn't sound very understanding of me and I wonder how that made you feel, because you haven't mentioned that at all.

PT: Well actually it's confusing, to be honest, but somehow probably not directly, somehow I sense you allow me choice. I don't know maybe I was wrong, but it's somehow I sensed it or allowed myself to sense this, so I went to this and umm, I was a bit disappointed, but I still think, err, I should have made this choice.

T: You allowed yourself, you have to allow yourself a choice, because I did not actively in so many words say yes, you should go, you must go, I will give you another session. All of that was unsaid because none of it was in fact talked about in the session. All the requests you made were out of the session time, but I feel like maybe there were nauseous feelings relating to me, for what I had done to you. Not giving you an understanding that you hoped I would.

PT: Hard, but ah, yes I felt something. It was going through my mind and through, ah, through me. I wasn't very well, that last session as well, and, umm, as I said I was more confused.

GAP

The patient described a vivid dream in which she was on her knees begging someone not to leave her for a day, and there were background voices saying: 'How can you leave her like that?" In discussing this, T says:

T: You have a nightmare where you are in a bleak vulnerable state and somebody you are looking up to, who should have stayed with you in that difficult state, is going away.

PT: I can partly answer, because it was the night before my birthday, so all my anxieties were there. Because every birthday before, something happened on the actual day. Again it was something you can help me with.

T: In the way you have spoken about it in the session, it sounds that what I should have been blamed for, you clear me of it. You hoped I'd be considerate and helpful and I was not. You say that you were confused by my response, but you are not upset about it or angry with me at all.

PT: Well, because you can't expect things from almost a stranger, it's not offended, err, not offensive, the same you expect from very, very close ones.

GAP

PT: ... Umm, but you say I'm serious about therapy, and what I'm trying to do outside the sessions is trying to think about many, many issues that are probably kept under the carpet or something. And, err, to think about issues in a new perspective and different ways than I did before, and I think it's very important. I don't know, I don't know whether my kind of conclusions are right or wrong, but the process of going through things is something clearly very important I think and ...

T: I think what you do in the session is that you do sweep things under the carpet and you would like these sessions to be like health and beauty "look good, feel good" sessions. There's something more disturbing, more troubling and much more distressing, as in the scene in your dream, lingering right there.

PT: No, no, no, but I'm not and to be honest I was surprised that I wanted to go to this actual "look good, feel good" session, because it's not like me ... [GAP] ... It's not difficult for me to expect some even unreasonable ... you know, denial or something like rejection from, from professionals, from strangers.

GAP

T: I think what you ... I think what has been important here is that you have again justified in great detail why you should contain your reaction towards me, why you should not be angry, why it is important for you to explain to yourself that what I did must be the right way to do things. I must have a good reason why I did what I did, even though it's left you confused and not sure what to expect, but you must at all costs contain that, because an over-reaction can be dangerous. Then what we see is that the next day, the next time for a session you are full of this nauseous reaction which you cannot explain.

The therapist also addressed how the patient could consider issues when she was alone, but they could not anticipate and think about them together.

Discussion

I highlight three things about these exchanges, aside from the obvious point that the therapist is explicit about, and clearly takes responsibility for, her part in the difficult communication that had taken place between herself and the patient (Item 15).

Firstly, the focus is on what happens, or has just happened, between patient and therapist in the session (Items 1, 3, 4, and 8, among others). The topic is events that in part occurred outside the session, namely communications between patient and therapist over changes in the sessions, but the central issue is how the patient deals with her feelings and tries to manage relations with the therapist *now*. T comments on how the patient is trying to keep a good atmosphere in the session, and how (taking up the patient's own words about herself outside the session) she is sweeping things under the carpet *in* the session (Item 11). Moreover, drawing on the content of the patient's dream, the therapist points to "something more disturbing, more troubling and much more distressing" behind what appears to be happening.

There is something here that I have not mentioned previously, insofar as much of the emphasis has been upon a therapist working on material derived from what a patient says or does or feels. However, psychotherapists are also attentive to feelings that are notable for their absence in given patients. Often these are not so much absent as stirred up in (sometimes projected into) the therapist. One simple example I recall vividly is how much work I had to do curbing the aggressiveness *I* felt towards a passive male patient who seemed to be devoid of aggression and helpless to do anything at all with the insights he gained. In the present case, the therapist is not working hypothetically, and the dream presents direct evidence of the kinds of disturbance and distress she can sense in this patient and that the patient needs to own if she is to manage her feelings differently.

Secondly, at times the therapist shows the patient the evidence on which she makes her judgments and suggestions (Item 9). She details the series of events over the changed sessions, and reflects how "that doesn't sound very understanding of me" (Item 5: a theme repeated at several points, such as "you hoped I'd be considerate and helpful and I was not"); she cites the nightmare as evidence of underlying emotional states; twice she refers to the way the patient had been speaking to her as if justifying the lack of blaming; and, as already mentioned, she takes up the patient's own description of herself as sweeping things under the carpet.

Thirdly, this psychotherapy illustrates what is meant by Item 2 of the Adherence Manual: "T focuses upon role relationships the patient is attempting to establish or avoid in the session." What the patient wants to establish is a good atmosphere of friendly cooperation and mutual accommodation between herself and the therapist. What the patient is trying to avoid is antagonism or confrontation, especially the possibility of expressing her own anger or blame towards the therapist, and/or finding out that indeed, this therapist on whom she depends can be thoughtless and disapproving. We do not know the details of why the emotional truth has to be suppressed, but the therapist begins work on the matter with her comment that "an over-reaction can be dangerous" and explores potential non-obvious implications through the example of the patient's nausea at the time of a session. Here we see the therapist addressing just some of the "ways in which the patient avoids, controls, or otherwise constrains intimate engagement with T" (Item 3).

Excerpt from third psychotherapy

The patient is a man with lack of fulfillment in life, in therapy with a male trainee.

T: I think when I asked you a question, I think you felt very angry.

PT: Which one?

T: When, when I asked for clarification about the scariness, you felt very angry when I interrupted you.

PT: I don't know if I was very angry, maybe just miffed.

T: Is that not … OK, because that might be a sort of point of clarification, but it might be part of the same process.

PT: What might be?

T: The qualification sort of takes you away from the feeling. So you've not got very angry, just angry or mildly angry, a bit more than mildly angry. So that process seems to defuse this sort of, takes the heat out of feeling.

GAP

T: I think again sort of something's happened. I think a few moments ago you sort of saw how serious things were, but I think through some process you end up in a position where you sort of lose contact with that.

PT: Yeah

T: And it seems like it's quite an active, sort of not meant to be seen, but I think it's quite an active process.

P: Yeah.

T: So something goes on from some kind of emotional contact, to some kind of masturbatory thing, I think. While we end up talking intellectually, I think what's really going on emotionally gets lost or attacked you could say.

P: Yeah, yeah I think that's right.

T: [two exchanges later] I think you're saying you feel you have some capacity to think about things that is good and creative and helpful, but I think you're also saying that you use that in a particular way, something called "analyzing," that actually can be used in a way that takes any pleasure out of your life, stops you from making contact with people, stops you from completing your work, and I think it's very active moment by moment in here as well.

Discussion

Like many of the excerpts considered already, this one illustrates the way in which, rather than asking questions, the therapist comments on what the patient is doing or feeling or communicating in relation to the therapist (Item 7). The therapist is doing his level best to pick up on what the patient has just said, done, or expressed (Item 8), and even when his comments do not quite capture the immediate present, they refer to the recent past of the session.

Centrally, the therapist is concerned to "comment upon manifestations of development or change in the patient's state and relatedness from moment to moment in the session, and perhaps over longer periods" (Item 10). The therapist not only manifests his "primary concern to explore the nature of the patient's state of mind and patterns of relatedness towards T," but also to "reveal the significance for the patient's everyday life" (both Item 13).

In analyzing the sources of development and change, the therapist "refers (directly or indirectly) to the significance of the patient taking or avoiding responsibility for his/her own thoughts, beliefs, choices, etc—especially within the session" (Item 12). He does this in at least three ways. Firstly, he persists in exploring feelings that the patient appears to disavow, especially anger. Secondly, he shows what the patient *does* to take the heat out of feelings, and actually pins down an instance in the patient's nit-picking over how angry he might have been. Thirdly, he stresses the patient's responsibility in being actively implicated in shaping what was happening, both in processes of "losing" contact and in disguising this activity ("sort of not meant to be seen"). At the same time, in remarking on the patient's potential ability to be creative and helpful, the therapist "addresses not only the negative/destructive side of the patient, but also the patient's wish and/or potential ability to make contact" (Item 14).

Excerpt from fourth psychotherapy

The patient is a young man, and the therapist a female trainee.

PT: How can I express it though, it's a feeling. It's not that I'm lost for words but how can I define it, if I've already defined it as standing still, being a little bit scared, confused, feeling the need to fill up that silence and it's not compared to meditation, because meditation is trying to empty your mind for a few seconds and focussing on something very relaxing and very peaceful and ...

T: It's difficult for you to be, to be with your feelings and be with another, just to be without action, without words.

PT: Because you're the person that would start sighing, then I would start sighing.

T: The other would lose interest.

PT: Would probably be concentrating on worries, and if there's that silence, I would do the same so there's no, there wouldn't be any connection, just the physical presence.

T: So in the silence I would go inside myself rather than remain connected with you.

PT: No, you would think about what I said, but it wouldn't be a work with two people, it would be what I would be feeling, because you cannot feel like, physically, what I feel. That's what I think ... A friend told me, why do you feel the need to fill up those silences, silences with standing still. The fact was that I was dying to fill up the silence, I felt very uncomfortable.

T: So the filling with words is a way of distracting yourself from the feelings inside you that you don't want. But I also think, a way of keeping the other engaged, perhaps there's a sense unless you work hard the other would disconnect and go into themselves.

PT: Yes, disconnection as well, but I would say, I would add one thing to see if the other person would lose interest as well, then I would be bored.

T: You would be bored?

PT: The other person would be bored as well with me. And also probably putting a lid on the voice that says, 'What am I doing here?'

Discussion

Although in this particular phase of the session, both patient and therapist are tending to speak in generalities, it is clear that each is aware they are discussing the therapeutic relationship. For example, the patient uses second-person and first-person pronouns when he says, "Because you're the person that would start sighing, then I would start sighing'"; and the therapist provides explicit anchorage when she says, "So in the silence I would go inside myself rather than remain connected with you." It should also be noted that, notwithstanding that most of the therapist's interventions are statements (she does also ask one question), her "major concern is with the *truth* of what is happening, especially in the session, and does not advise nor condone nor condemn" (Item 16).

The therapist weaves compassionate comments on the patient's defensive use of words to fill silence, with a willingness to hold the patient's hand as he explores the underlying threat that he might find *her* not only disconnected but also bored. In keeping with the emotional weight of the session, the patient finds a voice to express his despairing thought, "What am I doing here?"

Excerpt from fifth psychotherapy

The patient is middle-aged woman, and the therapist is a man similar in age.

T: There are different levels of things and one of the things which I think is still really important is to do with you trying hard, I think you try terribly hard, genuinely …

PT: Yes, 'cos you gave me a, sorry to interrupt, but you gave me a look last time when I left. As I looked back, you gave me this kind of a look and you probably can't remember it, but it was kind of, it made me feel like a naughty girl, you know like, like, it's almost like I've forgotten to hand in my homework or I'd neglected to do something and you, you know you gave me this slightly quizzical, concerned, almost despairing look as I left. It made me almost go on to giggle, but then I … then there was a big gap and I thought, Oh gosh she's, thought I didn't, you know … I, I, it was almost like there was an omission of some kind in that last session.

T: In the look there's a kind of … already in the look from me and the way you portray it looks as if it's, well, distanced. And I'm looking at you as a person who's either transgressed, done something wrong, or something, but with me slightly distanced from you, as you leave. And then what you do in thinking about it is: "Oh, gosh, oh gosh, he thinks this, he thinks that," and in both sets of experiences, you have the experience and you think I'm actually kind of disapproving … or, what else did you say?

PT: Quizzical.

T: You see, quizzical is already a bit once removed from you going off out of the door. And then you have your thoughts about "Oh, gosh," but something again quite personal, actually if one takes the description you give of my face, a lot of those things are very disconcerting. And here we are struggling in a way that is important for you. On your leaving it's as if I'm doing something to you which distances you from me and from all the more personal things that are going on. And then you think about them, "Oh, gosh is he disapproving?", and you come back after a long break and you try hard. You try hard to present something interesting and to get things going again.

PT: Yes, yes.

T: All I'm trying to say is this: There are times when I think you do feel more personally involved.

PT: Yes.

T: But things can interfere with that, where you, as it were, half step back … you have your ways, like you came today, almost as if I was unfamiliar, you were trying to present yourself again …

GAP

T: … Actually, you have these anxieties in a variety of circumstances, and they express something deep about you. And what I'm saying is in describing things in the way you did [at the beginning of the session], you were indeed managing them in a certain way, even as you told the story. The story was as it were keeping certain things …

PT: But I've always managed it that way. Those plates in the air have always been there, since I was at an age when I shouldn't have had to be spinning plates.

T: I think you are very attached to doing that.

PT: Yes, yeah, well I'm not surprised though, really.

T: Now what you do also say which I think is much more personal, is that you don't know how, you don't know how to come back after a long break and what that means, and get personal with me. You don't know how to do it. You do your best efforts and then you feel I find fault, saying that is not good enough, and you think, "Whatever I do is never any good."

Now when that falls away, when you stop spinning these things and I can see you've stopped, when you get over the fact you feel I've put you down, and particularly when I say that something is serious … it alarms you, you pull faces, because you feel I'm pushing something at you rather than taking something seriously, with you. Then it becomes possible for something different to happen and partly you feel relieved that at least you don't have to organize our getting in contact. And then one can begin to think about you as a whole person, including somebody as extremely sensitive to other people's reactions to you … whatever was on my face, you know you're very alert to these things. And you also hear me differently when you shift, you feel more with me.

PT: Yes, I do understand.

T: Yes, it's visible, I can actually see it. Yes, I can see when you shift.

Discussion

It seems unnecessary to labour how, in a more extended manner than in the first transcript of this chapter, this excerpt illustrates many of the principles of Brief Psychoanalytic Therapy. Perhaps in the forefront are the therapist's efforts to explore how the patient experiences him in the transference, but he also tracks shifts in the patient's relations with himself, he highlights the contrast between deeper and less intimate contact between them, he acknowledges how the patient is trying hard as well as evading things, he dwells on her emotional states and her responsibility for choosing to "spin plates," and he is serious in his commitment to pursuing, with the patient herself, what is emotionally true about her. These themes characterize almost all the therapeutic work presented in this book.

I conclude this chapter by noting that in the final transcript, as to some degree in all the vignettes, we see exemplified what appears as Item 17 of the Adherence Manual, which states, "T's manner conveys that *everything matters*. T's predominant attitude is of taking things seriously, especially things the patient is inclined to shrug off." More specifically, under the subheading "Overarching features of therapist stance," Item 13 reads: "Overall, T's primary concern is to explore the nature of the patient's state of mind and patterns of relatedness towards T, and reveal the significance for the patient's everyday life (rather than to make interpretations about links with the past, although these may occur)." Perhaps this is a suitably straightforward way to articulate not only the overriding concern of the therapists represented here, but also the psychoanalytic core of Brief Psychoanalytic Therapy.

Chapter 9

Is Brief Psychoanalytic Therapy distinctive? A research study

Introduction

Now for something completely different: a formal study of therapeutic interventions in Brief Psychoanalytic Therapy (BPT). The aim of the study was not to examine the effectiveness of treatment, but rather to explore whether the therapeutic approach has distinctive qualities. Of course, there are innumerable psychotherapies with which BPT might be compared but, to make a start, we explored similarities and dissimilarities with another relationship-based brief psychotherapy, Interpersonal Therapy (IPT: see Chapter 2 for details). In this chapter, as in Chapter 2, it makes sense to use the acronyms BPT and IPT, respectively.

I say that "we" explored these matters, and at the outset I need to acknowledge that the study was a team effort. Foremost among my collaborators was Maxine Dennis, a colleague trained as an IPT therapist as well as a psychoanalyst, whose many contributions included constructing the IPT adherence scale and manual. Claire Pocklington, a medical student at the time we embarked on the study, researched adherence manuals. Marisa Velazquez helped with the initial database, and she, Andrew Colitz, and Lisa Cohen served as diligent raters. All these individuals pitched in with ideas as well as energy, and I do thank them all.

I begin by outlining the rationale for our research. First, I shall say why we conducted the study at all. Second, I shall explain why we conducted the study in the way that we did.

Background to the investigation

Why go to the trouble of designing, implementing, and analyzing a study of what happens in BPT? After all, the principles of the clinical approach have been laid out, and therapist reports and transcripts have revealed how different BPT therapists engage with patients in moment-to-moment transactions as well as over the course of psychotherapy. What is to be gained from an empirical study that tries to pin things down and condense meaningful clinical work into numbers? Frequently such investigations yield only crude collective data that obscure the varieties and subtleties of clinical phenomena, whether these concern patient characteristics, therapeutic interventions, or clinical change. Who would bother to read a report of the study? In short, who cares?

These rhetorical questions have some weight. Before I respond to them, I should point out that substantial parts of this book have been concerned with the BPT Treatment Manual and Adherence Manual. The manuals would not have been written, were they not needed for a research project. Yet, so far, the manuals have served a purpose beyond that of research, namely to specify what BPT involves. I hope the contents of previous chapters illustrate how it is not necessarily the case that research instruments blunt our sensitivity to clinical phenomena, even though they may do just that. On the contrary, systematized descriptions of BPT have alerted us to features of the approach that we might otherwise have overlooked or taken for granted.

As a matter of fact, this book would not have been written had a study not been planned. It was only as I began to think about investigating the approach that I realized we would need a specification of what BPT is, and a means to recognize when BPT and not some other kind of treatment was being delivered by therapists. Sessions would need to be recorded. Scientific considerations left no alternative but to distill and in due course to list the essential elements of BPT, and then to make verbatim recordings of patient–therapist transactions. The benefits turned out to be substantial, and not only for the formal research.

This was not a surprise. In conducting research, as in other areas of life, one tries to avoid spending time doing things that serve only as a means to some other end. Whatever the outcome of the study in terms of formal results, my colleagues and I wanted to learn things as we went along. The transcript material on which we were working, as well as the BPT Manual and Adherence Manual to which I was devoting attention, promised to reveal things to ourselves, never mind anyone else, about our theoretical preoccupations and the clinical work we hold so dear.

Here, then, were good reasons for embarking on the study. We were ready to be challenged not only to think more deeply, but also to translate our thoughts into measures that might yield meaningful data. We realized there was much we did not know, and we were interested in finding out more. Being far from confident about the suitability of conventional scientific methods in this context, we became interested in seeing whether it would prove worthwhile to conduct a particular style of investigation into our therapeutic work.

Such personal interests were complemented by wider aspirations. We had been, and continue to be, deeply concerned about the vulnerability of psychoanalytic psychotherapy. One source of vulnerability is that, although there is substantial empirical support for a variety of short-term psychodynamically informed treatments (Chapter 2), such evidence is often sidelined or disparaged by those who espouse other forms of brief psychotherapy intervention. It is deeply regrettable that psychoanalytic psychotherapy is given so little respect by so many, and the situation needs to be addressed on a number of levels. We felt that we could make a contribution by characterizing Brief Psychoanalytic Psychotherapy, illustrating its potential value through practice-based evidence, and laying the groundwork for future research.

First steps

In the investigation of the process or effectiveness of any treatment, it is necessary to establish the precise characteristics of the treatment being administered. If researchers are studying the effects of medication, for example, they need to establish whether or not the correct form of medication is being prescribed and consumed in accord with the recommended dosage. Otherwise, they might draw conclusions about the high or low effectiveness of a treatment, when in fact the treatment was not administered appropriately.

These principles apply to the evaluation of psychological therapies. As we have seen, psychodynamic treatments vary in explicitness of therapeutic focus, therapist activity and guidance, homework, frequency of sessions and length of treatment, as well as in more subtle but no less important aspects of therapeutic technique. If researchers are comparing two such treatments, they need to evaluate whether in their sessions with patients, clinicians are adhering to manuals outlining the principles of each. This means that independent raters should assess recordings of sessions in relation to criteria drawn from treatment manuals, and the inter-rater reliability of their separate ratings established. In order to avoid bias, raters should be unaware of which treatment they are rating.

Therefore the first step was to characterize BPT in a Treatment Manual. This sets out what the treatment comprises. It distills the approach. The second step was to write an Adherence Manual. This lists elements of treatment in such a way that a clinician can read the transcript of a session, and score the degree to which any given element of BPT was or was not a feature of the transcribed session. Similar treatment and adherence manuals were constructed for IPT. Then two separate, independent raters evaluated transcripts of audiotaped sessions of treatment conducted by therapists who were well-versed in the principles of the treatments administered. Transcripts were mixed up together, and raters were not told which of the two treatments they were rating in any given script. The procedure enabled us to assess whether the ratings were consistent, and therefore whether they provided a basis for drawing conclusions about what was objectively true of the therapeutic interactions as captured in the transcripts.

Methodological issues

To evaluate treatments delivered by different therapists, transcriptions of a single audiotaped session from each treatment were transcribed. In fact, this was the only session of the 16 sessions of treatment that was audiotaped. Patients' permission for the recording was secured at the outset of treatment. There is little doubt that to audiotape psychotherapy affects what happens in treatment, and therapists were aware they would need to address the significance of the procedure in the psychotherapy itself. For whom was the recording made? How secure was confidentiality? Was the treatment mostly a vehicle for research? And so on. For the specific purposes of evaluating therapist interventions, we made the assumption that patient–therapist transactions recorded in a selected session would be sufficiently true to the remainder of what transpired, and to what the brief therapy would have been like without any recording, to justify using this material as representative of the conduct of treatment.

Audiotaping and then transcribing sessions has a number of practical advantages, not least flexibility for the subsequent timing and location of the work conducted by raters. However, transcription is time-consuming and expensive, as is adherence rating. Given that in any case we were keen to avoid taping more than one session, it was necessary to select which of the 16 sessions was to be recorded. The problem here is that therapeutic activity is likely to change as treatment proceeds. In IPT, in particular, early sessions involve more structured therapist–patient interactions than later ones. Therefore we decided that for each treatment we would record, transcribe, and rate a session after the first phase of treatment was over, mostly around the eighth session. Once the sessions from seven BPT treatments and seven IPT treatments had been anonymized and transcribed, they were systematically randomized in order before being given to raters for evaluation. Therefore raters were unaware, at least at the outset, which treatment they were rating.

There were seven different psychotherapists, one for each of the seven BPT cases. The rationale was that, in this way, we could assess the consistency in the delivery of BPT across therapists. If the work of just one or two therapists had been studied, we might have been evaluating the style of those particular therapists. The same procedure applied to IPT treatments. We did allow that one or two therapists who were trained in both approaches could serve as one of the BPT therapists and also one of the IPT therapists. There were three raters, one who rated all the scripts and two others who rated either earlier or later transcripts. This meant that every transcript was rated by two independent raters, each of whom had experience of dynamic psychotherapy. They piloted and discussed ratings on practice transcripts before embarking on the study proper. Raters were aware that they probably had a mix of IPT and BPT transcripts, but were unaware of how many of each, or in what order they were presented.

Now it is necessary to consider in more depth issues that arise in rating adherence. I have touched upon the complex relation between thinking about clinical practice on the one hand, and research methodology on the other. Consider this issue with regard to adherence ratings. The principle seems to be simple: investigators devise or adopt measures of what BPT involves, then they apply these measures to data from clinical sessions. The measures should reveal whether, or to what extent, any given treatment conforms to the principles and practice of BPT.

The picture becomes more complicated when one questions the assumption that the BPT adherence measure does indeed measure what it is supposed to measure. Perhaps the items of the measure are too vague to allow independent raters to agree in their ratings. Perhaps they are insufficiently precise to discriminate between one treatment and another, with few items that are specific to the conduct of BPT. Maybe only a subset of the items of the Adherence Manual might generalize across BPT treatments conducted by different therapists.

Given the modest scale of the study and the preliminary nature of our research, it was impossible to address these challenges fully. Yet even with the small numbers of patients and therapists we could recruit, it might be possible to get a handle on several of the most important issues. One reason is that, even if there were a risk of imprecision in the measures, the principal danger was that they would be insufficiently powerful to reveal differences between treatments. If, in the event, clear differences emerged, it would be very unlikely that the results could be explained as artefactual. In addition, as already discussed, we evaluated whether independent raters could agree in their ratings of therapeutic transactions. If they could, then we would be in a position to test whether their ratings revealed specificity to what happens in BPT.

For determining treatment specificity in ratings, it would have been inadequate to devise a BPT adherence scale and apply that to the two treatments. The BPT adherence scale is new, and it was not possible to conduct the kinds of formal analysis of the scale to establish its consistency or test-retest reliability, or the validity of its contents. Therefore treatment-specific BPT and IPT scales were supplemented with already established rating scales that were relevant for psychodynamic treatments. While these scales were not particularly sensitive to the specific qualities of BPT, they were helpful in providing complementary measures of similarities and differences between BPT and IPT.

Therefore in evaluating transcripts, we ended up with a set of adherence measures that were even-handed in relation to BPT and IPT: a specifically BPT adherence scale, a specifically IPT adherence scale, the Interpretive and Supportive Technique Scale (ISTS), and the Vanderbilt Therapeutic Strategies Scale (VTSS).

So much for devising and selecting the measures. In an ideal world, it would have been preferable not only to have more therapists giving each treatment and therefore more transcripts to evaluate, but also to have had different raters for each rating scale. Otherwise it is open to doubt whether, once embarked on ratings with one rating scale, a given rater might be influenced in how he or she scores the next rating scale, and so on. Given that our resources were limited to having two raters per transcript, we could not ensure that the ratings for any given transcript were fully independent of one another.

In order to reduce the potential impact of this limitation, raters used the four different adherence ratings in random (albeit not strictly randomized) order. In addition, once estimates of inter-rater reliability had been completed and it came to comparing treatments, the BPT scores of rater 1 were used for the evenly numbered transcripts (which had been randomly numbered for the order in which they had been rated) and the BPT scores of rater 2 were used for the unevenly numbered transcripts. Then the IPT adherence scores of rater 1 were used for the unevenly numbered transcripts, and those of rater 2 were used for the evenly numbered transcripts. When it came to the analyses, then, for a particular transcript a given rater's score for *either* BPT adherence *or* IPT adherence was employed, and not both. This does not fully dispel concerns that some of the ratings might have been affected by previous ratings a rater might have made, but it does mean that for any given transcript, the analyses were conducted with BPT and IPT ratings made by different raters, not the same rater.

Procedure

Patients selected for the study had primary diagnoses of recurrent depressive disorder or depression (eight cases), anxiety (three cases), or unspecified neurotic disorder (three cases). Although formal comorbid diagnoses of personality disorder were rare, the majority presented with long-standing difficulties, nearly always extending over five years. There were five female and two male patients in each treatment group; those in the BPT group were aged between 36 and 55 years (mean 43 years), and those in the IPT group were between 37 and 60 years (mean 45 years).

There were five female and two male BPT therapists, of whom four were senior staff and three experienced trainees. There were six female and one male IPT therapists, of whom three were senior staff and four were experienced trainees. They understood the principles of applying the respective approaches within a 16-session time-limited framework. Those therapists still in training received supervision of their work.

One session around the middle of each therapy was audiotaped, with patients' permission (which was sought prior to the commencement of treatment), and transcribed. The transcriptions were rated by two independent raters, using four adherence measures.

Measures

Each of the 14 transcripts were given to two psychodynamically informed raters to evaluate in their own time. The raters were instructed that to begin with, they should read through and think about a given transcript as a whole. Then they should go back and examine the text in more detail, and employ the four adherence scales, in any order (which was not consistent within nor across raters—in retrospect, we should have randomized this systematically), to score whether items were characteristic of the therapist's activity. Each scale comprised a list of succinct items intended to capture aspects of therapeutic intervention. Each of the scales was accompanied by an adherence manual that explained, with examples, what the items meant. In what follows, I employ the abbreviation T for therapist.

BPT adherence scale

This scale comprised 17 items, and was accompanied by the BPT Adherence Manual described in Chapter 7. On a single scoring sheet, the items (grouped under three separate headings, as in the Adherence Manual) comprised the brief sentences listed as numbered items in Chapter 7. Each item was to be scored on a scale from 0 (not at all characteristic of T's stance) to 4 (highly characteristic) in relation to the transcript under review. By way of a reminder, here are two examples of items from each grouping:

Focus on patient–therapist relatedness

- T tracks specific patterns of *interpersonal interaction and/or relation* between the patient and T.
- T addresses the ways in which the patient avoids, controls or otherwise *constrains intimate engagement* with T.

Specifics of therapist technique

- T tends to pick up on what the patient has just said, done, or expressed.
- T comments upon manifestations of *development or change* in the patient's state and relatedness from moment to moment in the session, and perhaps over longer periods,

Overarching features of therapist stance

- T addresses not only the negative/destructive side of the patient, but also the patient's wish and/or potential ability to make contact.
- T conveys, directly or indirectly, that T's major concern is with the truth of what is happening, especially in the session, and does not advise or condone or condemn.

IPT adherence scale

We were unable to locate a published adherence scale for IPT that was suitable for our purposes, so we devised one in a style that was in keeping with the BPT scale. Elements of the scale were adapted from Tactics and Techniques sub-scales of a much longer adherence and quality scale constructed by Stuart (2009). As I have said, my colleague Maxine Dennis, who is trained in the delivery of IPT, took a leading role in constructing the IPT adherence scale and writing an explanatory manual to accompany it. Once again, each item was to be scored on a scale from 0 (not at all characteristic) to 4 (extremely characteristic) of the transcript under review. Here are six illustrative items from the IPT scale:

- T links symptoms and current interpersonal context—that is, translates features of depression/anxiety into feelings that arise in/as a result of current personal relationships in outside life, and vice versa.
- T discusses an interpersonal formulation with the patient, where "formulation" is a coherent description of pattern(s) of relationship with others that captures how difficulties arise in day-to-day interactions.
- T conducts a communication analysis. This means that T focuses in blow-by-blow detail upon the patient's pattern of communication with other people, and the patient's feelings about such interactions. This may feature a hypothesis about what leads to communication difficulties.
- T elicits/discusses affect, taking up and clarifying the patient's feelings as these emerge in the session.
- T links "content" and "process" affect, where "content" refers to feeling experienced outside the therapy, and "process" refers to feelings emerging with the session (not necessarily feelings towards T, although these would count).

- T engages in social skills training such as exploring more effective social behavior.

There were two additional scales. These were intended to capture, firstly, a potential contrast between supportive and interpretive aspects of treatment, and secondly, general aspects of interviewing style vis-à-vis a specific focus on patient–therapist transactions.

Interpretive and Supportive Technique Scale (ISTS: Ogrodniczuk and Piper 1999)

The ISTS was, in the authors' words, "designed to measure interpretive and supportive features of technique for a broad range of dynamically oriented psychotherapies" (p. 142). The purpose of employing the ISTS in the present context was to determine how far BPT and IPT compared and contrasted in being "supportive" or "interpretive," features of therapeutic approach that were somewhat more general than those targeted by the BPT and IPT adherence scales.

The ISTS is accompanied by a manual for the scale, providing definitions of the items and illustrative examples, as well as a treatment manual. There are 14 items, the seven odd-numbered items describing supportive features and the even-numbered items describing interpretive features. Each is scored from 0 to 4. Whereas in the original scale, scores accord with the "emphasis" given to features, we kept to our "not at all characteristic" to "extremely characteristic" terminology. The full scale appears in Ogrodniczuk and Piper (1999, p. 154). Here are examples of items that followed the introductory clause, "The therapist attempted to:"

Supportive

- gratify the patient, i.e., make the patient feel good rather than anxious in the session
- make noninterpretive interventions, e.g., reflections, questions, provisions of information, clarification, and confrontations
- engage in problem-solving strategies with the patient, i.e., generating and evaluating alternative solutions to external life problems.

Interpretive

- maintain pressure on the patient to talk, e.g., by at times remaining passive, by not breaking pauses, by not answering questions
- make interpretations
- make links between the patient's relationship with the T and the patient's relationships with others.

Ogrodniczuk and Piper (1999) report high inter-rater reliability for the full ISTS scale and sub-scales, as well as data on internal consistency and factor structure.

Vanderbilt Therapeutic Strategies Scale (VTSS: Butler, Henry, and Strupp 1995)

This scale contains one set of items to evaluate aspects of a psychodynamic stance or style (12 items), and another set of nine items designed to capture a specifically interpersonal focus that characterizes manualized Time-Limited Dynamic Psychotherapy (Strupp and Binder 1984). In the latter TLDP-specific respect, the authors explain that the principles are: "(1) assessing patients' pathological interpersonal functioning in terms of cyclical maladaptive patterns and (2) the therapeutic task of identifying and addressing these problematic patterns as the emerge in the therapeutic relationship" (p. 631). The full VTSS appears in Butler, Henry, and Strupp (1995, p. 632), along with evidence of the adequate psychometric properties of the measure. In the present study, we had raters score on a scale of 0–4 (rather than 1–5 in the original) to accord with our other measures.

Examples of VTSS items are as follows:

Psychodynamic interviewing style

- T encourages the patient to experience/express affect in session.
- T responds to the patient in accepting/understanding manner.
- T responds to the patient's statements by seeking concrete detail.

Specific strategies

- T encourages the patient to explore feelings/thoughts about T/the therapeutic relationship.
- T uses own reactions to some aspect of the patient's behavior to clarify communications/guide exploration of possible distortions in the patient's perceptions.
- T addresses obstacles (e.g., silences, coming late, avoidance of meaningful topics).

Results

Adherence scales

The first set of results concern estimates of the degree to which independent raters agreed in their separate ratings of the transcripts. Inter-rater agreements were excellent with regard to total scores on both the BPT adherence scale and the IPT adherence scale (in each case, ICC = .93). Agreement was good on the two parts of the ISTS scale (for supportive, ICC = .74, for interpretive ICC = .69) and on the "specific strategies" sub-scale of the VTSS (ICC = .87). With these particular transcripts, inter-rater agreement was near to zero on the "interviewing style" part of the VTSS, so this will not be considered further.

Given that the BPT adherence scale was a major focus of the study, further analyses were conducted on the sub-scores of this scale. Inter-rater reliabilties were excellent for the "relatedness" and "specific techniques: sub-scales (ICC = .94 in each case), and good on the "overarching features" sub-scale (ICC = .75). To evaluate whether the three sub-scales of the BPT adherence measure were consistent with each other, we used the subset scores that contributed to the total scores used in the group comparisons (below). When a transcript was scored high on "relatedness," scores on "specifics of therapist technique" and "overarching features" were also high (Pearson correlations r(12) = .91 and .82, respectively), and there was also a strong correlation between "specifics of therapist technique" and "overarching features" (r(12) = .92). This indicated substantial consistency across the three BPT sub-scales.

Comparisons between treatments

In what follows, I cite significance levels as calculated by Mann–Whitney tests, but the group contrasts are self-evident from the ranges of scores reported. On BPT adherence scales, there was a highly significant group difference (p < .001). On this measure of BPT adherence, the range of the BPT transcript scores was between 37 and 58 (mean 48.7, where the maximum possible score for both BPT and IPT scales is 68), and the range of IPT transcript scores was between 10 and 23 (mean 15.0). Therefore every single one of the BPT transcripts scored more highly than every one of the IPT transcripts.

On IPT adherence scales, there was again a highly significant group difference (p <.001). The range of the IPT transcript scores was between 27 and 51 (mean 37.4), and the range of BPT transcript scores was between 8 and 21 (mean 15.4). In this case, then, every single one of the IPT transcripts scored more highly than every one of the BPT transcripts.

The profile of results on these two measures is depicted in Figure 9.1.

Results on the two sub-scales of the ISTS again yielded a distinctive profile for each mode of treatment. Compared with IPT transcripts, BPT transcripts were rated as significantly *more* interpretive (p < .01) and significantly *less* supportive (p < .001). More specifically, on the interpretive sub-scale of the ISTS, all but

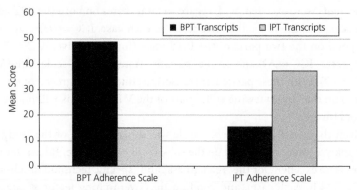

Fig. 9.1 Transcript scores on BPT and IPT Adherence scales.

one of the BPT transcripts were scored more highly than the highest-scoring IPT transcript. On the supportive sub-scale, by contrast, every one of the IPT transcripts scored more highly than the highest-scoring BPT transcript.

Finally, on the "specific psychodynamic strategies" sub-scale of the VTSS, there was again a highly significant group difference (p < .001), with a complete split in scores from the two forms of treatment. All the BPT transcripts scored highly (range 17–26, mean 21.1), whereas all the IPT transcripts were given low scores (range 3–9, mean 6.7).

Discussion

The results from this study were clear-cut. For the BPT and IPT adherence scales, there was very substantial agreement in the ratings of independent raters. Moreover, the three BPT sub-scale scores correlated highly with each other. It was clear from visual inspection of the BPT sub-scales that each was making a substantial contribution to the overall rating. Inter-rater reliability for scores on the ISTS sub-scales and the "specific psychodynamic strategy" sub-scale of the VTSS were also good.

Secondly, all seven transcripts of BPT sessions were given higher BPT scores than the seven transcripts of IPT sessions. Here it should be recalled that, for the purposes of the analyses, any given transcript received a BPT rating from a single rater, randomly selected from the two individuals who had made ratings, and IPT ratings on that particular transcript were made by the other rater.

This latter consideration is also relevant for the next finding, namely that all seven transcripts of IPT sessions were given higher IPT scores than the seven transcripts of BPT sessions. Therefore it was not just that one of the two treatments scored highly on everything, a result that might have reflected, for example, how active and interventionist one group of therapists had been.

On the contrary, there was specificity to the profile of results. BPT transcripts were scored high on BPT adherence *and* low on IPT adherence, and IPT transcripts were scored high on IPT adherence *and* low on BPT adherence.

The nature and magnitude of these differences between the two forms of treatment attest to the degree of homogeneity within each group. Different therapists were conducting BPT in a similar way, and different therapists were conducting IPT in a similar way. The contrasts were not specific to particular therapists. Given that potential interference effects across different adherence measures is likely to have been modest, the major methodological limitation of the study concerned the small number of transcripts being rated. As it turned out, marked consistency in the results, with high within-group homogeneity and very substantial between-group differences, provides unexpectedly strong indication that the BPT and IPT adherence measures would have yielded similar profiles of scores if substantially more treatments had been rated.

The distinctiveness of BPT was also apparent in the ratings from the remaining two adherence scales. The ISTS scores revealed substantial group differences on the "supportive" sub-scale, where BPT transcripts were scored very low and IPT transcripts high. This provides evidence that BPT therapists were withholding forms of supportive or reassuring intervention that IPT therapists provided. Yet again, this was not because BPT therapists were less active overall, because they scored highly on the interpretive scale. Rather, they were more occupied with commenting on what was happening in the transference. This is also reflected in the final result, where they were rated highly for employing strategies specific to psychodynamic therapy with its focus on the interpersonal, patient–therapist relationship.

In the light of these results, it becomes difficult to sustain the view that all therapies are much the same. True, IPT is not the closest relative of BPT, so the contrasts are unlikely to be quite so stark if, say, BPT is compared with DIT or the Conversational Model. Here it is relevant that the BPT adherence scale seems to be reasonably successful in capturing essential features of the therapy. If this is so, how far does it *look* as if other treatments such as those described in Chapter 2 would be given high scores on the BPT adherence scale?

Of course it remains to be studied whether, if different forms of brief psychoanalytic psychotherapy have distinctive characteristics, they have distinctive effects (for some patients, when administered by some therapists). Here it may be worth adding that in the experience of raters of the transcripts, IPT and BPT *could* be very different from a patient's point of view, but the contrasts became less striking when experienced and sensitive clinicians were therapists. There is much that remains to be understood about the interaction between different therapists and different treatments.

Conclusions

The empirical study I have described provides evidence that in all likelihood, BPT is distinctive. The BPT Adherence Manual comprises items that can be rated reliably, and on the face of it, many of these appear to characterize BPT more than they apply to other psychodynamically informed treatments. The quantitative comparison demonstrated that there are certainly contrasts between BPT and IPT. More than this, the results indicated an impressive degree of consistency among BPT therapists in conducting psychoanalytic psychotherapy in a style that conforms with BPT principles. From a complementary viewpoint, the consistency in scores on the BPT adherence scale suggests that the items succeeded in capturing something essential to BPT. Other investigators' adherence measures yielded additional evidence for the claim that prominent among the characteristic features of BPT is a focus on the transference.

At the end of the day, we have achieved some clarity over what BPT involves. This has been made explicit, both in outline as a Treatment Manual, and in fine-grained detail as an Adherence Manual. Critics may be skeptical of BPT, and supporters enthusiastic—but neither of these groups can be in doubt over the nature of the treatment about which they disagree. From here on, anyone with the necessary resources, commitment, and skill is in a position to conduct research to uncover what the evidence has to say about BPT and its value.

Chapter 10

The course of treatment

Introduction

It is time to reconsider the course of Brief Psychoanalytic Therapy with individual patients, and to integrate the minutiae of patient–therapist exchanges within a broader perspective. It goes without saying that a patient's experience is of paramount importance in psychotherapy. The reason for honing therapeutic technique is to enrich that experience in the service of enhancing the person's well-being and promoting his or her development. A danger of focussing on a therapist's emotional stance and interpretative activity is that one can shift attention away from the task of taking on board, and being committed to addressing, the needs of *the person* in treatment.

As I discussed in Chapter 1, a therapist is ever thoughtful about the lengthier relationship within which here-and-now patterns of relatedness are situated. The therapeutic relationship has its own characteristics, its own shape, its own deep significance. This is true, whether one is thinking of the patient's relationship with a therapist as an assessment consultation unfolds, or a relationship with the therapist that spans weeks, months, or years. A therapeutic focus on the immediate present should implicate and reflect awareness of this larger canvas.

I trust such breadth of vision has been evident in the clinical work described earlier, and will be apparent in the two cases that follow. Here the vignettes are intended to capture how a devotion to analyzing the transference need not, and should not, stand in the way of being attentive to the evolving relationship, not least in relation to its imminent ending. In the two cases to be described, the development of the therapeutic relationship over time was profoundly important for, as well as an expression of, the respective patients' emotional growth and integration.

First case vignette

Ms D was a woman in her late twenties referred for low mood, feelings of anger, guilt, and being out of control. She had had a variety of childhood difficulties, and had received psychiatric medication for attention difficulties in childhood. She had also experienced frequent moves of home with her family.

Ms D had not returned her questionnaire prior to the initial consultation, but brought this with her and explained it was very difficult for her to fill out. She wrote about herself in neat, small capital letters, and in some detail. She described how her brain whirrs, but is "generally numb." She contemplates self-harm. She becomes bored by herself, extremely frustrated, and very angry. She can feel exposed to others, wishing to run away. Ms D's account of her family included reference to her conflictual relationship with her father.

The initial consultation

I began this interview just over 20 minutes late, because for some reason, the appointment was not in my diary. Even as I greeted Ms D from the lift, there was initial hesitation between us and I think she corrected my pronunciation of her name. She looked grim.

Once in the consulting room, I apologized that Ms D had been kept waiting. I said that if she could stay, I would make up the time so she did not lose part of her interview. She asked, half rhetorically, what had happened, did I forget? She went on to say that it had been a battle to get here, her experiences of the NHS have been difficult … and for a long time things have been an emotional struggle for her.

I said how it had affected her, being kept waiting. She became tearful, and said that she had an acquaintance who tried to kill herself, and came here and was faced with someone not saying anything, and this friend said nothing either. Ms D wondered what she would feel if the same thing happened to her. She added that she doesn't know why she is crying.

There was a feeling of great emotional pressure within the room. On the one hand, Ms D conveyed how difficult it was for her to contain her own feelings, both of need but also of frustration and anger. Her reference to finding a therapist not talking was only very partially justified in relation to myself, because in fact I had already said quite a lot (note: this last comment reflects how I felt defensive in the countertransference). There was a masochistic tone to her comments, and she seemed at first to be pushing her state at me, as if I should need to be made to register her feelings. Yet even at this stage, I did not feel unduly intimidated or put on the spot.

Although it is difficult to recall the order in which Ms D described things, she did communicate how she is a person who tries hard with others, but always seems to be doing things they don't expect or don't want. She conveyed how she can be forthright in what she says, and not always tactful. She told how her father had high expectations of her that she never fulfilled. She also described how she made herself unpopular at school, for instance by not cow-towing, and she recalled telling a prefect that respect has to be earned.

As Ms D was to comment later, it felt like being in a pressure cooker, and I made reference to this pressure. I said that despite this, it seemed important that I didn't react immediately to her direct questions about my coming late, or to her implying that I might be silent, when in fact there is a story behind each of these things. So, too, when she produced the questionnaire, I thought it was important that I did not presume why she had not sent it before. She said she did not quite know what I meant about there being a story. I explained that I meant she needed more than a reflex or pre-packaged response. For someone to understand her, it would take time and attentiveness. I might need to be direct over her forthrightness, but also aware of her vulnerability and distress.

Ms D then talked at some length about childhood illnesses and her long-standing attention difficulties. She described her father as successful but something of a bully towards her, and her mother as someone who did not stand up for (and was even mocking towards) Ms D. She also described how in the present, she can feel numb at times she should be caring toward people.

What I have not conveyed adequately is how Ms D remained very much on edge as she gave her account. She would be tearful and then half-laugh at herself or other people, occasionally making throwaway remarks or commenting on herself negatively. She communicated an intense mix of distress, anger, and frustration, not least with her own capacity to fire off with feelings of one kind or another. She described how she has been called an unguided rocket. So, too, she expressed upset at how she cannot manage, and how other people have to get it just right in order to be there to help her.

I took up some of this in relation to her engagement with myself. For example, I said at one point that not only was she acutely sensitive to my stance, but also she was very much at war with herself. She said that's true, but then moved away to what was almost a soliloquy about her difficulties in feeling things. I took up how this kind of move away leaves her isolated with her problems, rather than remaining in contact with me. It was difficult for her to feel understood, beyond an experience that lasted just a few moments.

What followed was a period of perhaps a minute when Ms D gathered herself together and became more coherent and settled. She was now in firmer contact with myself, and at this point, perhaps paradoxically but also appropriately, she commented how she does not know how to stay with feelings. I pointed out that yes, she can move away from contact. Yet it is becoming evident that she can use what I say to gather herself together, and make a more personal connection.

Then there was another shift as Ms D started to berate herself that she lacks the discipline she needs to organize her chaotic life. I took up how she takes a particular view of what is needed, and the kind of discipline required. In fact, what we have seen here is that when she feels firmly taken in hand, but also understood, she changes. I said that what she now demonstrates is how she can show a lack of sensitivity and compassion toward herself. She is clearly aware of how unsatisfied and unsatisfying she feels herself to be.

I asked Ms D whether she dreams. She described a recurrent dream in which she was alone and being pursued or looking for something. I asked her whether she thought this had significance. She responded in a rather distant way about her wish to find escape. I felt her attitude toward herself, and the lack of depth to her emotional register, were rather typical of other parts of the session. Having said this, she did seem to follow me when I pointed out the emotional impact of what the dream depicted, that is, her being all by herself, running, being pursued, and also seeking what she cannot find.

Toward the end of the interview, I felt Ms D moved away once more. She seemed to experience my own comments as requiring an explanation from her, rather than communicating understanding. In tears, she said I must understand she does not trust me, and she does not want to expose herself and then be left with that. I took up how what she says is true, but there is also a way in which she does trust me. Her response was to offer a partial correction, saying that she is coming to respect me. She clearly appreciated how we had got hold of some important things, and I felt considerable respect for Ms D's own ability and willingness to become reflective and thoughtful.

For our follow-up consultation, Ms D arrived on time. I told her we had half an hour for this meeting, and she looked at me in silence for a moment and then asked what was going to happen. I said that perhaps she might tell me something of her experience last time. She said she found it surprisingly good.

What Ms D then conveyed was how that first meeting had been emotionally intense and important for her. She commented that at last she had found someone with the analytic skills to enable her not to run circles around the person. She also said how she had so many thoughts and feelings, she did not really know where to begin in this brief time. I acknowledged the importance of our first meeting, and again, she registered with some relief that I was taking her on board. I also said how it is really impossible in this brief meeting for her to convey all that she feels. She said she definitely wants to pursue this form of psychotherapy. She added that she knows she needs help, and it is not other people's fault if they do not really see her. She agreed when I pointed out that here she was also indicating an agenda for herself, namely to present herself honestly when she could. After some discussion, she decided to take up the option of brief psychotherapy with a colleague whom I much respect, and who I knew had a vacancy. At the end, Ms D said how, although she does not often say this, she wished to thank me and say it was good to meet me.

The course of treatment

Ms D's female psychotherapist was an experienced and able clinician who had trained as a psychoanalyst and was well versed in shorter forms of therapeutic contact. From the outset, this therapist was sensitive to how Ms D felt her mother had withdrawn in her early childhood, at a time when Ms D had suffered early physical illness. The therapist was also aware how, when Ms D was given medication for attention difficulties in early childhood and then later in adolescence, she had experienced this as something that was meant to stop any complaint, effectively substituting for as well as blocking out any acknowledgment of her anger and unhappiness. The psychotherapist was concerned that a brief intervention carried the risk of triggering feelings in Ms D to the effect that no-one could bear to stay with her and remain in contact with her emotional states of distress, pain and rage.

At the beginning of the therapy, the therapist felt that although there was genuine and moving contact between herself and Ms D, this tended to be fleeting and swiftly followed by movement away to other thoughts or to concerns with other people. When the therapist commented on this or other shifts in therapeutic engagement, Ms D seemed to register an impact but then move away once more. The therapist would often feel emotionally involved and concerned in a maternal way, but then she would feel her interpretations were pushed back as Ms D seemed impelled to diminish the therapist's importance to her. Ms D insisted that the experience of being left was "just life" and that she simply needed to get on with it. She also had a tendency to treat herself harshly, admonishing herself for her feelings on the one hand and her defensiveness on the other.

The quality of the therapeutic contact can be illustrated by a mid-therapy session in which Ms D began by saying she had been procrastinating all morning, wasting time when she should have been getting on with important things she needed to do. She has a long list in her head that she should probably write down but then she can't work out what is important. The same is true for here—with all the things she thinks she should talk to her therapist about, she doesn't know what is important. Then there is this panic of not knowing where to start. She will probably just bury herself in some completely mindless, totally time-wasting and mentally destructive activity.

The therapist suggested that perhaps this was also an anxiety that they might not make real contact and instead get caught up in something mindless, going round in circles. Ms D corrected this, saying not in circles, but maybe by the end of the sessions she will still have all this stuff. Anyway, life is like that. She has spent so much of her life procrastinating, and she thinks to herself, "Well why don't you get off your lazy arse and do something."

The therapist took up how this demonstrated a kind of whipping of herself that served to move her away from anxiety about what was happening in the immediate present. Perhaps her remarks were not so much about whether they could cover everything, but whether they could really make contact in a way that actually makes a difference. Ms D responded by agreeing that the thing is to make contact. She needs to connect with someone, because the self that others see does not always correspond with the self she lives with. This led her to talk about a relative who told her she was a horrible child over her entire childhood. Then she became silent, seemingly lost in her thoughts. The therapist took up how this seemed to be a moment when something over-whelms Ms D inside, and she loses contact with herself as well as the therapist.

Here is a brief near-verbatim excerpt from the recording of that session:

PT (PATIENT): I've never lived in one place for a long time. I've never had to be with the same people or in the same environment for very long.

T (THERAPIST): So really, not knowing what it's like to stay and to let someone know you for a long period of time.

P: Not in close proximity. No. ... I feel really sick.

T: And I wonder whether something of that sickness is because you're trying to stay right here and talk to me about things that are clearly very painful and difficult to talk about.

PT: I don't know how, I've never stayed before.

T: And yet here you were staying. Staying with me right now talking about these things.

GAP

P: ... It's strange to realize I'm scared. Being in one place ... or probably, part of my issue with my partner is that he is not going anywhere, but even as hard as I try to make him go somewhere sometimes, he's not going anywhere.

T: Hmm. That's the point, isn't it? Not just being in one place. It's being in one place with someone else.

PT: Yeah. Absolutely.

The therapist felt that making, losing, sustaining, and staying in contact, regulating distance both with what Ms D felt and with the therapist as someone who could take this in, were the critical issues addressed repeatedly over the course of psychotherapy. The means to alter such engagements, not least the control Ms D could introduce by attacking herself or inviting such attack, were also firmly in focus. It was certainly possible and fruitful for the therapist and patient to make links between such issues and Ms D's history and the significant figures in her past and present, but detailed attention to the struggles with the therapist seemed vital for deepening contact as the psychotherapy progressed. Ms D did come to trust her therapist more, and was able to distinguish between the planned ending and simply being left with too much to cope with alone. As the therapy ended, she expressed her gratitude, and described how she felt she had been taken seriously and had her difficulties acknowledged. She also said she hoped for more treatment at a later date, and anticipated returning for a consultation with Dr. Hobson.

Follow-up

I saw Ms D for a follow-up consultation some weeks after she had ended her Brief Psychoanalytic Therapy.

Ms D arrived on time, and said how the treatment with her therapist had been helpful. She conveyed how she had ended up feeling much better in herself, but then qualified this by saying of course this could have been the result of other changes in her life. I took up this qualification in relation to her hesitation in realistically but also generously crediting herself with having made good use of the sessions. She referred to how she is better in asking for things she needs. I was reminded (and reminded Ms D) about an issue that had arisen in the assessment consultation, to do with her being at war with herself. It seems that war is not the only option.

The principal theme of the session was how important it is for Ms D to tease apart her different strands of feeling. This was an alternative to letting some feelings obliterate others, or condensing into an unmanageable knot her resentment, frustration, assertiveness, aggression, and more vulnerable feelings such as love or need. So, when she admitted that she still finds me intimidating, I acknowledged this as part of the truth, but also said that it needn't prevent me having access to very different sides of her personality.

As it turned out, this was to be the first of a series of intermittent meetings between Ms D and myself, woven into a period of some months that included significant events and changes in Ms D's life. I found Ms D a more direct and multi-faceted person than previously, even though she would sometimes lapse into more stereotyped roles. She could express her hurt at people finding her "difficult"; although she does not come easy, that does not mean she is just difficult. She had genuine insight into how she can marginalize feelings, or sometimes (as she expressed it) wallow in them. Even in widely spaced meetings, it was possible to sustain work on how she can feel dumped with others' feelings, how she feels other people are not available to help, and how she cannot trust her own ability to communicate in a way that resolves things.

It was very moving to witness how Ms D had changed, and how much more satisfaction she was gaining from life. I felt we were both enriched by our contact.

Second case vignette

Ms E was a woman in her late thirties who was referred with states of anxiety. Her background included an unsettled family life, with traumatic early separations.

The initial consultation

Ms E brought her questionnaire with her to the assessment consultation. Her appearance was somewhat plain and serious. She began by giving an articulate description of herself, sometimes with theatrical gestures to punctuate her story. She had had substantial psychotherapy in the past. The content of what she said was mainly concerned with her states of anxiety and panic, when her hands sweat and she can feel tingly. These states were sometimes occasioned by financial worries, or by anxiety over the whereabouts of family members when they were not in sight.

However, there was little indication that Ms E really registered the implications of what she was saying. I felt I was hearing a well-rehearsed description, partly constructed to engage and entertain me. Indeed, in the early part of the interview there was little to indicate Ms E's own expectations over what I might do to help her. She explained that she comes to find some way of getting round her difficulties, or to control them.

I had been quiet for some minutes, and now I remarked on how Ms E seemed to be familiar with her anxieties from early in life—she described how in childhood, she had got into panics thinking about death—but also, how she was used to telling her story. Initially she felt negatively judged and "stupid." She conveyed hurt that of course she had to explain her situation, what else could she do? Bit by bit, however, she became more thoughtful. For example, I took up how she had conveyed that her previous therapy had been helpful, but this was on the basis of changes she observed from a somewhat detached viewpoint. There was little she had said about it deepening her understanding of herself. Also I remarked on how some of the things she said were clearly personal at some level, and showed a degree of insight, yet it was not clear how deeply she engaged with the issues.

Ms E said she could see what I meant. Here she flushed and rather to my surprise, became more emotionally available in a way that, though fluctuating, remained essentially intact for the second half of our meeting. There were a number of themes that emerged, in particular Ms E's quickness of mind that she would apply to her problems, in the belief that this would resolve them. In fact, there was something missing in her own relation to herself as a vulnerable, childlike, anxiety-ridden individual. Instead of encompassing this within herself with sensitivity and firmness, she presented herself as someone with uncontrollable anxiety states that needed more effective treatment (and she referred to the fact that she is on antidepressants). As I said to her, what seems to be missing within herself is just the kind of understanding, containing relationship she feels was missing through the difficult part of her early life.

There were additional subtleties to this picture. For example, Ms E said how when she was very small, she used to do things like bite into cups or retreat to her room. Ms E admitted she could be intolerant toward others, especially when threatened. In addition, she has difficulty in thinking things through. She mentioned how in her previous psychotherapy, she was resistant to the process in some ways. In this meeting with myself, she struggled to go beyond her too-quick formulations to achieve deeper thought.

Having said this, there was something impressive about Ms E's ability to acknowledge the truth in what was being uncovered. She was able to admit how childlike she feels, and spoke of how she has evolved her way of talking in order to get a reaction from others. As I pointed out, getting a reaction is very different from receiving understanding, and it appears she does not feel that understanding is available for her. At several points in our exchanges, it was uncertain whether she would take some matter seriously, or short-circuit her thinking processes and move on.

When I asked Ms E whether she dreams, she said yes, all the time. For example, she has dreams of flying. She likes to fly away, she commented. But then she couldn't keep it up. She seemed to understand when I drew attention to the way this captured the early part of our meeting.

Overall, it was important to discover that Ms E could listen and feel understood. When I asked her about the feelings with which she came today, she became rather impatient. She said that of course she came with all kinds of feelings, from being pessimistic to hoping there might be some help … and added that she found it very difficult to fill in the questionnaire. Once again, I was struck by the relative accessibility of more complex and authentic ambivalence in her underlying feelings.

For our follow-up consultation, Ms E arrived on time. She said that she felt peculiar leaving our last meeting, and confused. Yet she also felt I had quickly got the measure of her. In fact, she had been feeling better since. She said she'd been thinking a lot, and trying hard to control some of her feelings.

I took up how Ms E presented two very different sides of herself. On the one hand, she is thoughtful, insightful, and appreciative of our meeting. On the other hand, she conveys how she was confused, and in her manner as much as the content of what she said, communicates how she does not really know where she is or what to do about it. We spent some time on how there is this gap between herself as thoughtful and intelligent, and another side to Ms E which is much less thinking and less able to commit herself to grappling with things. She may be articulate, engaging and entertaining, but at the same time she may be flying out of contact with things within herself that are more emotional. Ms E said she appreciated being challenged. She also referred back to our first meeting, and said it had been helpful.

I outlined how cognitive-behavioral therapy offers one strategy to address her difficulties, in that it may help to circumscribe and then deal with important issues. After much thought, I also said she could have brief psychotherapy with myself. I left her to think this over and get back to me. In the event, she asked to see me.

The course of treatment

Early on, Ms E said how she does not know what to provide for me. She feels she has to talk if there is a silence, to fill in. I said she feels it almost doesn't matter what she says, as long as it fills in—which means the problems are articulated, but not dealt with; they hover there unresolved. She paused and was quiet. Then she said that last time she felt stripped, naked and humiliated. It's not like her other experiences of therapy when she could chatter on. I said her chattering on keeps at bay her really having to confront things that are painful or difficult. I also said how at one moment she could feel I was on her side, helping her, but very quickly she could feel pointed at, found fault with, unattractive (her word) and stupid (again, her word). Correspondingly, she can half step back and carry on thinking all by herself.

When next we met, Ms E said she felt very angry about the previous session. It was like I kept saying that what she was doing was wrong. I batted away things she wanted to talk about, I didn't want to hear. I don't know what her life is really like! She felt bullied.

I took up various aspects of this. What came across was not only Ms E's anger with me, but also her feeling of trying to provide something that was always felt to be wanting, and of not being listened to. As she said of another context, she wants to be vindicated. It turned out that she had actually felt that *I* had been angry and impatient in the last session.

Ms E settled as the session progressed. At one point, movingly, she said she is lonely, and after a brief silence, shifted stance and said she had dried up.

From the outset of the following session, Ms E seemed more available. She began by saying that she's always afraid that what she might say is wrong, so had had to prepare herself and what she's going to say. Once she went to Italy and tried so hard to memorize Italian, she couldn't listen to what the other person was saying, and what she herself said was crap. It was horrible. I took up the importance of what she was expressing. I pointed out that when I repeated her statements to her slowly, she could begin to think about how personal were the issues of which she spoke. Yet as she talks about them, it would be so easy for the meaning to be lost, in her own mind and mine.

It had become a central matter for the psychotherapy, to distinguish two very different communicative states. In one, Ms E would talk *about* herself from a position that was at one remove. In the other state, she was less guarded and more direct and thoughtful, even when this provoked anxiety and sometimes prompted her to cover herself. As I took up with Ms E, she can wish to escape not only because of her fear of criticism, but also her difficulty with intimacy. At the same time, I felt she was on for the task of psychotherapy, and was going for it.

Here is a part of a transcribed session, relatively late on in the psychotherapy, when Ms E had returned from a three-week break. Ms E had begun the session by saying she didn't really feel like coming today:

PT: It must have been the big break and I felt OK ... and I felt, I didn't feel like I was seeing all the negatives I suppose, because things have been going well and I haven't been, I haven't been thinking about myself very deeply. I didn't think I had much to say, but I did have an interesting thought on the way here.

[Ms E proceeded to give a long, rather laboured account of times when she has and has not had anxiety attacks in the past, and told a tortuous story of difficulties the family had with neighbors.]

T: The first thing is that there's been a big gap and you come here and you tell me that in a way, things have been relatively OK. You've mixed feelings about coming, particularly about looking at negative things. In a way you've reached an equilibrium that's working OK. You have mixed feelings about upsetting that.

PT: Because things are going OK, you know.

T: Things are going OK and yet you know the states that you can get into. You describe very difficult conditions that you cope with well, I mean as much as anyone can, and begin telling me about it as if these were your symptoms, your anxiety attacks coming specifically at certain points ... [other material] ... I'm just saying what you bring is really important, about you getting on a certain plane, and the plane is one where you think a bit, you find things interesting and you bring things to say, but if one really asks is this getting you somewhere new, is this ...

PT: Yeah, but I would blame that on you really, because there's been such a big gap and I think when we come week after week after week, then we get into a bit of a different thing. You know and it's hard when there are big gaps.

T: Let's go back to that, because that is much more direct. [Discussion ensued about the forthcoming ending of therapy.]

Then later in the session there occurred the following exchange:

PT: I do see you kind of reel me in, in the sessions a bit. It's almost what you kind of described, kind of reel me in, you know, and I don't know quite what the, I don't know what that means for me, really.

T: There are two things, one is ...

PT: I value, I value how it happens. I've always known that it was a sort of a short thing, and I couldn't put too much, you know, invest everything in it.

T: No, but you invest a lot. There are two things. One is you're right about reeling in. The other is reeling in to where.

PT: Yes.

T: But the point is that actually you know you value this, you know I'm trying to work for you.

PT: I do.

T: And it's going to be a big loss, when you don't know what's going to happen. Not just the reeling in process, which I think is really important, but also the feeling of you arriving at a place where you can be more yourself, which is both you as a child and as a grown-up. And yes, you can be quite judgmental, yes, you can be sharp, and that's all part of it, more to the good. What you clearly conveyed today was returning to a place and state with me, not newly finding it. And it's one thing about how you're going to reel yourself in, and another knowing when this is the real thing, this is what intimacy is.

In these later phases of the psychotherapy, I was impressed how Ms E could introduce complex and reflective ideas as difficult-to-articulate thoughts of personal importance. She herself spoke of her feeling that there had been a shift in herself. There was also development in what became available as a complement to Ms E's feelings of being judged negatively, namely a side to herself that is judgmental, impatient, even hateful—and in the session, I felt she was actually rather cold toward her own coldness. Despite this, Ms E had a much fuller presence, and it became possible to unpack (for example) how rather than feeling guilty about her hostility and impatience toward others, she is more disquieted.

Now I move to the final session. Ms E initially began by saying that she seems to have the options of being barking mad here (and she admitted to being quite attached to her oddball persona), or earnest and dull. Yet, I said, I did not think she felt my experience of her was of a dull person. So clearly there are other options. She told of a dream in which her house was shared with one of her neighbors, and they were replacing the light switches with more modern and aesthetic ones, perhaps illuminating things. But also there was this other person who occupied one of the rooms. I asked whether Ms E was taking the dream and her thoughts about it seriously. She said she was. The session concluded with our looking at Ms E's anxieties when dealing with others, and how firm I had had to be with her, to respect both her vulnerabilities and her need to be assertive. It was a moving session.

In her client satisfaction questionnaire, Ms E wrote that what was most important to her in the psychotherapy was the therapist's "honesty and perseverance. He made the best use of every second of every session." She felt treated with respect, and believed she had become kinder to herself. She recorded that she was very satisfied with the treatment and its ending.

Discussion

By now, a reader could be forgiven for wondering whether much of psychotherapy is about discerning and addressing how a patient deflects from intimate contact, or how he or she substitutes non-developmental forms of relatedness for those that might lead to mutuality and satisfaction. Although this would be too sweeping a generalization, there is much truth in it. Surely, then, it is justifiable to ask: Why should people presenting with anxiety, or depression, or fatigue, or medical preoccupations, or difficulties in sustaining work or relationships, or a variety of other complaints, all need help with achieving intimacy?

I hope that the clinical vignettes from this chapter, as well as those from earlier in the book, suggest answers to this question. Let me summarize the principal reasons.

We all need the support and availability of other human beings. We may have an image of ourselves as independent, but this is largely illusory. To exist as adequately functioning individuals, we need to be listened to, understood, shared with, and supported—not to mention, loved. Even when alone, we exist in relation to others in our minds. From a psychoanalytic perspective, internal versions of interpersonal relations actually structure the mind, so that our very capacities to think and to manage our emotional lives are founded on relations among person-like mental agencies within us. But even at a common-sense level, if we are limited in our capacities to turn to, communicate with, and take succour and other vital input from others, then our personalities and emotional lives are going to be constrained and very likely troubled.

This is only the beginning of the story. Psychoanalysis has revealed how what is lived externally in relation to other people and what goes on among person-like agencies within our minds are intimately related. In the transference, a patient relives in relation to the therapist patterns of relatedness and relationship rooted in the past and repeated again and again in personal engagements. The patterns reflect what the patient carries and has to bear within his or her own mind, all the time. Not only this, but an optimal means to development and change in a person's internal world resides in analyzing those patterns as they are lived out in relation to the therapist in the transference. If a therapist can be sensitive to what a patient experiences and expresses in fragments, or what a patient cannot bear, then the patient is in a position to internalize—that is, take in from his or her experience in the relation with the therapist—fresh capacities to integrate and manage feelings, and sometimes new abilities to think. These changes can have a profound influence on how the patient relates to him or herself, as well as toward others. I hope the vignettes in this chapter have illustrated something of this process.

It would be extravagant to claim that all mental disorders have deep underlying commonalities in being expressions of relational disorder, or that this is all there is to consider in the pathogenesis of psychological dysfunction and distress. What about the impacts of poverty and physical disease, for example, never mind the relevance of genetics for mental disorder? Yet it is far from clear how justified and helpful it is for conventional psychiatry to ascribe a plethora of comorbid neurotic conditions and/or a bewildering array of so-called personality disorders to given patients, as if they have a stack of concurrent medical diseases. There is a tendency to underestimate the causal influence of social developmental factors in the origins and persistence of psychological dysfunction, and the roles such factors play in configuring the variety of expressions of mental distress.

I believe it is often by following the course of a disorder over time—whether by adopting a lifetime perspective on the genesis and perpetuation of a person's difficulties, or by tracing the details of a person's development through their inhibitions, conflicts, and distressing states of mind in dynamic psychotherapy—that we learn more about the nature and diversity of mental disorder and suffering. In so doing, we also learn something of how psychotherapeutic relationships facilitate change.

Chapter 11

The place of Brief Psychoanalytic Therapy

Introduction

In previous chapters, I have outlined what I believe to be a potentially valuable psychoanalytic style of brief psychotherapy. Here, in the concluding chapter of the book, I shall reflect on the origins of Brief Psychoanalytic Therapy and its place among other psychological therapies, as well as issues of training and supervision.

As conceived and articulated in this book, Brief Psychoanalytic Therapy exists because colleagues and myself—psychoanalysts and trainees who had experience of conducting both longer-term and relatively brief (one-year) psychoanalytic psychotherapy—felt it would be feasible and potentially helpful to apply psychoanalytic principles in 16-session psychotherapy.

Of course, we were not alone in taking this stance, and other clinicians have evolved brief psychodynamic psychotherapies of different kinds. But on this occasion, I was leading the charge. My reasons for doing so included the fact that for many years, I had been conducting assessment consultations according to psychoanalytic principles (as discussed in detail in Hobson 2013), and this had seemed fruitful. I had been supervising relatively brief treatments along the same lines. I saw no reason why a similar approach could not be used for a range of interventions, whether of six sessions, 16 session, or 116 sessions, providing one respected that each would need to be recognized as having a beginning, a middle, and an end. In the case of brief interventions, the end should be pre-specified, held in mind, and addressed from early on in treatment.

Therefore it was in the context of service delivery in the UK National Health Service that I began to formalize Brief Psychoanalytic Therapy. Within the NHS, pressures to reduce the costs of health care, as well as to limit treatments to those that have a widely acknowledged evidence base, threaten the provision of dynamic psychotherapy. Often on inadequate grounds, NHS decision-makers have come to view longer-term psychotherapy as self-indulgent and unjustified, and other forms of psychodynamic psychotherapy as scientifically questionable. It is widely held that only through fairly drastic modification can something psychoanalytic be retained within shorter forms of psychotherapy.

It was this prejudice that colleagues and myself wanted to challenge. *If* a brief psychotherapy is all that can be offered to someone needing psychological help, does it follow that the therapy should *not* be one conducted according to psychoanalytic principles? In our view, it does not follow. Our first tasks were to document how a short-term treatment can hold to a consistent psychoanalytic rationale, and then determine whether it could be beneficial for a number of patients.

With these aims in mind, a small group of consultants and trainees in the Adult Department of the Tavistock Clinic came together to form the Brief Psychotherapy Workshop. As I acknowledged in the Preface, my colleagues Maxine Dennis, Jo Stubley, Gabriella Rubino, and Malika Verma were hugely important in developing and sustaining the enterprise. I wrote the BPT Manual to represent a style of thinking and working with which we were all familiar. Now we were in a position to recruit additional therapists from within the Department who said they would be prepared to see patients within the constraints of Brief Psychoanalytic Therapy. No wonder there were those who had misgivings about the undertaking. I shall consider three prime concerns, because these should trouble anyone conducting brief dynamic psychotherapy.

Doubts and uncertainties

To begin with, there was unease about the brevity of treatment. A number of therapists were skeptical over what could be achieved in 16 sessions. Surely, too much would remain unaddressed. It seemed implausible that 16 sessions would be enough to work through a person's long-standing difficulties and emotional habits of mind. Besides this, there was a serious chance that patients would feel picked up and then dropped, perhaps repeating trauma that would differ from patient to patient, but in each case lead to harm. Was the approach really in the patient's best interests?

Secondly, there were anxieties, especially among trainees, over whether therapists could actually deliver what was needed. Brief Psychoanalytic Therapy seems to require swift and incisive work in the transference. As a therapist, it is difficult enough to work out what is going on in the therapeutic relationship. Substantial time and supervision may be needed. Then one has to formulate what to say and when to say it. A trainee might be clumsy as well as off-target, yet in any brief treatment there is pressure to do something. What is to prevent a therapist from provoking a patient's dismay and distress,

and stirring up unmanageable feelings? The idea of jumping in to such intimate engagement is all very well, but it is scary. Is it also irresponsible?

Thirdly, there was the matter of selecting patients for treatment. Who might
benefit from treatment, and for whom might it be harmful?

Let me address these issues in order.

Firstly, the matter of brevity. One needs to *remain* skeptical about how
much can be achieved in 16 sessions, or indeed in lengthier treatment. Yet as
case histories illustrate, a lot can happen over this time span. Within the clinical descriptions I have given, it is possible to discern developmental progres-
sion in how patients felt and thought about themselves. There was indication
of meaningful, step-by-step change in the way they made choices over their
emotional conduct. Although we do not know how far such developments
continued after treatment had ended, clinical experience suggests that "brief"
is not always the same as "too brief."

Still one can press the question: Is it in the patient's best interests? This
partly depends on what alternatives are available. For some patients, certainly, longer-term treatment is preferable, and brief therapy comes in as a
possible second-best. For others, psychodynamic treatment of any kind might
be inappropriate. For example, patients with serious emotional difficulties
who have achieved reasonable compromises in life may be given support to
sustain their ways of coping, rather than invited to begin a potentially destabilizing therapy. Yet there might be a number of individuals for whom Brief
Psychoanalytic Therapy is optimal. Here it is worth remembering that longer-
term psychodynamic treatments have their own hazards, beyond the expend-
iture of time and money. One characteristic of Brief Psychoanalytic Therapy,
as I think most of my colleagues would agree, is that it is bracing. Both therapist and patient know they need to get on with things. This concentrates minds.

There is also the fact that brief treatment can lead to longer treatment. If a
patient is brought to the point of seeking longer-term help, or if some additional support is needed for a period in order to consolidate change, then all
to the good. What I do not recommend, is to suggest at the outset that Brief
Psychoanalytic Therapy is a preliminary to longer treatment. It should be a
discrete treatment in itself, with its own shape and ending.

The termination of psychotherapy is a critical phase for almost all patients
in treatment. A patient may have feelings of many kinds, ranging from painful loss and gratitude to resentment over abandonment, and of course such
emotional states may be managed or defended against in an infinite variety of
ways. If both patient and therapist can be honest about the significance but also
the limitations of what treatment has achieved, and address a patient's strong
feelings about being left with so much still to manage, then this can prove a

significant bulwark against reversion to the *status quo*. The ending needs to be anticipated, and then faced. What happens subsequently is a separate story.

A second set of misgivings concerned the delivery of treatment. Especially when they first engaged in Brief Psychoanalytic Therapy, trainees felt anxious about what they *should* be doing. As psychotherapy progressed, and with supervision, this attitude began to change. It was gratifying how younger therapists who initially had felt at sea developed an aptitude for the approach, even over the course of a first treatment. True, it required discipline from both therapist and supervisor to maintain a close focus on the transference in the context of a time-limited structure of 16 sessions. The work was rewarding, but also taxing.

One element of the process deserves emphasis. By and large, it seemed that if therapists were prepared to commit themselves to addressing the patient's difficulties as manifest in the transference, then often patients were able to use the therapist's firmness to make real progress. I can think of a number of cases where once the therapist acquired the conviction that development and change were possible within the scope of brief treatment, even when only a few sessions remained, then at that point the patient developed and changed.

These considerations prompt the question: What does a clinician need to bring to Brief Psychoanalytic Therapy in order to apply its principles appropriately? Is the approach suitable for clinicians early in their training? More than once I have pointed out that the treatments reported in this book were conducted by staff who had substantial clinical experience and theoretical knowledge to inform their work. Whether therapists in the early stages of their training could or should attempt to deliver this form of therapy is doubtful, in my view. Training is just part of the story, of course, because much depends on a given therapist's personality and giftedness for the work. I do not know whether there are some trainees who could take to the approach relatively early on in their careers, but I would need to be convinced this is a good idea. My experience is that most trainees take a long time to understand what it means to work in the transference. Then there is the extra challenge to apply this understanding in brief work.

I would like to re-frame, and then leave open, the question of training, from a complementary viewpoint: For what kind of clinician—how trained, how experienced, how flexible, how supervised—might the principles of Brief Psychoanalytic Therapy be helpful in providing a kind of strategic point of orientation? The idea contained in this latter question is that far from being a starting-point for a therapist, the approach may be a vehicle for the implementation of the therapist's already-existing therapeutic capacities and knowledge. This was, after all, where Brief Psychoanalytic Therapy began.

Finally, there is the question of how to select patients. To this question we do not have an answer. Thus far, all we have to go on is the clinical evidence provided in this book. What I have not illustrated, partly because I did not have the patients' permission to present material, are cases where the treatment was *un*helpful. I have known very few such patients for whom this was the case (from an admittedly small and selected sample), but it is likely that there are many for whom the approach would be unsuitable. We just do not know. Our approach at the outset was to exclude patients who were not interested in this way of addressing their difficulties, those whose degree of disturbance led us to think the treatment would be destabilizing, and those for whom the brevity of the treatment might be traumatic, for example patients with multiple separations. Broadly speaking, most individuals we took on tended to have a mix of (what are called) depression and anxiety, as well as difficulties in work and relationships. The cases described in the book are more or less representative. Further discussion of how one might approach the task of assessing individuals for treatment appears in the book, *Consultations in Psychoanalytic Psychotherapy* (Hobson 2013).

Now I return to the question of whether it is justifiable to give this treatment the title of Brief Psychoanalytic Therapy. I shall consider two sides to this question. Firstly, is it really appropriate to use the term "psychoanalytic"? Secondly, is the treatment sufficiently distinctive to warrant a proper name?

Wherefore psychoanalytic?

At the end of the day, does it matter whether Brief Psychoanalytic Therapy is psychoanalytic? It is what it is.

I think it does matter. The essence is to work in the transference, and working in the transference is what psychoanalysis is about. If one wants to learn more about the kind of clinical orientation that Brief Psychoanalytic Therapy involves, or about the kinds of clinical phenomena to which one needs to be sensitive, or the kinds of therapeutic challenge that are likely to be generated by different kinds of patient, then it is to psychoanalytic literature and to psychoanalytic supervision that one should turn. From a complementary perspective, it would be disrespectful as well as dishonest if one claimed that the approach was anything more than a spin-off from psychoanalysis.

Beyond providing an initial, highly synoptic overview (Chapter 1), I have not dwelt on many theoretical issues from psychoanalysis that are relevant for Brief Psychoanalytic Therapy. I have made scant reference to Freud's wide-ranging explorations of the unconscious (top of my list, the early pages of Freud's 1917 paper, Mourning and Melancholia), and paid almost no attention to the content of patient's phantasies and object relations (impressively discussed by Ogden 2002) that underlie forms of a person's social experience as well as his or her defensive manouevres (Isaacs 1948). I have not considered the significance of dreams as a means of access to unconscious processes (Freud 1900) and an avenue for clinical exploration (e.g., Hobson 2008; Perelberg 2000; Segal 1981). Perhaps of even greater concern, given the centrality of unconscious interpersonal communication and defence for psychopathology and psychic development, is how little I have discussed mental processes of projective identification and containment (Bion 1962a; Feldman 1997; Joseph 1989), or what, from a different standpoint, Winnicott (1965b) described as the "holding environment." Diverse forms of human vulnerability and destructiveness, perversion, and defensiveness have been set to one side as I explicated a particular therapeutic orientation. However, these matters have not been absent from the thinking behind what I have written. For those coming fresh to psychoanalytic psychotherapy, they are topics to be pursued through the psychoanalytic literature and other avenues of clinical and theoretical learning.

To repeat what I have said before: There is little or nothing original in Brief Psychoanalytic Therapy. This is not a branded approach. Nor is it compiled by someone wishing to integrate all that is good in dynamic psychotherapy. It is simply a distillation of selected psychoanalytic principles that lend themselves to application in short-term psychotherapeutic work.

The word "selected" is needed here, because the chapters of this book—and *a fortiori*, the BPT Manual and Adherence Manual—leave out much that would need to appear in any adequate account of psychoanalytic technique. There are very many considerations, from arranging the setting to adjusting technique according to circumstance and patients' degree of disturbance and capacity to symbolize, from integrating work on positive and negative aspects of the transference to beginning and ending treatment, from drawing on a patient's history to making links with the patient's presenting difficulties, that have been neglected here. Even the here-and-now focus advocated in Brief Psychoanalytic Therapy needs to be set in broader context. Although current patient–therapist relatedness needs to be ever-present in a therapist's mind, this does not mean that all the therapist says and does has direct reference to the present intersubjective exchange. There is a lot more that needs to feature in treatment.

To put this another way, if Brief Psychoanalytic Therapy were *solely* based on the techniques described in the Manual, and if the therapist had little other clinical, theoretical, or psychodynamically relevant personal resources on which to draw, then this would be a very impoverished mode of therapy. Certainly, it would not deserve the adjective "psychoanalytic." Insofar as one wishes to think of Brief Psychoanalytic Therapy as an "it," then one might say that it assumes as its background substantial clinical and theoretical knowledge. From this perspective, what the Manual does is to specify significant but not sufficient ingredients of the treatment. The nitty gritty is a certain style of working in the transference that draws upon a therapist's sensitivity to the countertransference, that entails compassion and respect for the patient, and that reflects a commitment to seeking after truth. But this is not all that a treatment of any given patient involves.

One cluster of issues troubles me especially. Some psychoanalysts would feel dismayed that in this form of therapeutic encounter, on the patient's side there is so little scope for classic forms of free association, and on the therapist's side, too little space for evenly suspended attention (Freud 1923). How could a therapist heed Bion's (1988, originally 1967) injunction to the analyst to approach sessions without memory or desire, when the therapist's mind is cluttered with a list of therapeutic principles and a deadline of 16 sessions? How can troubled patients follow a drawn-out developmental trajectory when hurried along by the clock's insistence, if not the therapist's over-zealous attentions?

To register the force of this critique, consider this condensed summary of a clinical paper by Coltart (1992, originally 1985) on the treatment of a transvestite. Coltart begins the paper as follows: "The analytical psychotherapy of this man lasted for just on three years … It fell fairly distinctly into three phases …" The first phase of approximately one year was characterized by intense engagement in which the analyst "often felt uneasy and rather suspicious of the subtle flair he demonstrated for the work … and I often felt impelled to point out to him that the acuity of his insights left his pathology intact" (pp. 28–29). It was only after a year that the patient began to gain real insight, and now some months of aggressiveness were followed by a period of difficulty and inertia, as well as intermittent heavy drinking. The patient became quite seriously depressed, and described feeling shattered. Subsequently this changed again, and for a while the patient became contemptuous and superior toward the analyst, then depressed again. Further ups and downs in the patient's states of mind occupied much of the final year of treatment.

Coltart gives a vivid account of the many different emotional and relational issues that needed to be addressed over the three years of this man's treatment (and see O'Shaughnessy 1988, originally 1981, for vicissitudes over a 12-year analysis). My point in offering this schematic description is to make a simple point: it seems inconceivable that a 16-session psychoanalytic therapy would have done anything more than scratch the surface of this patient's problems, never mind work through issues in depth. Coltart was explicit about her reservations over the outcome of the longer therapy she had provided, despite all that had evolved in the course of treatment.

Brief psychotherapy is not the same as psychoanalysis. It is not for all patients, even for all those interested and amenable to a psychodynamic approach. It does not give scope for the kinds of careful, detailed—but by no means slow nor languid—progressively and gradually unfolding analytic work that I have just illustrated. Consider now a different aspect of this same problem.

Here my clinical material comes from a paper in which Ogden (1994) discusses how often one needs to analyze "the matrix of the transference-countertransference," before symbolic meanings are addressed. By the matrix he means a patient's way of thinking, talking, or behaving. This orientation is, of course, much in keeping with that of Brief Psychoanalytic Therapy. But sometimes it entails that the analyst needs to relate to a patient, perhaps over an extended period of time, in a manner very different from that which characterizes brief treatment. Ogden describes the treatment of a patient Ms L who presented with emptiness and despair, as follows:

> Days, weeks, and months went by during which I said practically nothing … Gradually, I came to realize that Ms. L. and I were not involved in the beginning of an analytic dialogue. Her words were not carriers of symbolic meaning; they were elements in a cotton wool insulation that she wove around herself in each meeting.
>
> In retrospect, it seems to have been of critical importance that in the initial years of work I did not succumb to my own wish to establish my existence in the patient's eyes by insisting that I be recognized as an analyst. Although I had not articulated this for myself at the time, I now believe that it was essential that I neither interpreted the patient's storytelling as an act of stubbornness or resistance to the analysis, nor engaged in countertransference enactments designed to allay the feelings of isolation that I was experiencing.

> (Ogden 1994, pp. 146–47)

I leave it to readers to reflect on this clinical account, because the implications are unsettling for anyone who wishes to practice Brief Psychoanalytic Therapy. The fact is, not only but especially in brief dynamic psychotherapy, a therapist might easily become too active, too focussed, too intent on analyzing this or that aspect of what is happening, to retain sensitivity to a particular patient's needs. For instance, a patient—and at times, *any* patient—may need a therapist who is quietly present and receptive, either for shorter or longer periods, not one who is talking a lot. The therapist, too, needs space to think and to associate to what is happening in his or her own mind (Bollas 1992). Although Brief Psychoanalytic Therapy requires a therapist to pay serious attention to such matters, the Manual does not stipulate as much. I trust these vignettes of psychoanalytic work exemplify what I have discussed as the kinds of clinical and theoretical understanding that constitute essential complements to, as well as a background for, the approach.

In summary, then, if Brief Psychoanalytic Therapy is psychoanalytic, it is certainly not psychoanalysis. If, as I have claimed, it distills certain psychoanalytic principles, it does not capture them all. Partly with this in mind, it should be adopted in a flexible way, especially in relation to a given patient's needs. The approach is built on psychoanalytic foundations, and this being so, therapists need to construct their own practice on this bedrock.

The specialness of Brief Psychoanalytic Therapy

Whereas I do not claim originality for Brief Psychoanalytic Therapy, I do think it is different from many other brief psychodynamically inclined therapies. Moreover, I believe its distinctiveness matters. On the other hand, I would hesitate to argue with the view that this book has done little more than illustrate what might be a significant *element* of psychotherapeutic work, providing certain technical considerations are borne in mind. By this I mean that in order to work in the transference, at least in the manner characteristic of Brief Psychoanalytic Therapy, it requires therapists to devote themselves to tracking moment-by-moment shifts in patient–therapist engagement. It seems to me that despite the consistent and coherent orientation of Brief Psychoanalytic Therapy, there is considerable latitude for given therapists to modify their stance according to choice. To practice the approach is not to apply the principles of the BPT Manual at each and every moment of the treatment. As I said earlier, the Manual is not prescriptive. Rather, it is intended to capture the *kinds* of focus and style of intervention that characterize this form of treatment.

One of the familiar ways to puncture enthusiasm about the specialness of an approach, whether clinical or intellectual, is for a critic to claim that others do or think the same. For instance, other kinds of therapist might insist: "We, too, adopt techniques similar to those you describe for Brief Psychoanalytic Therapy." For good measure, and tellingly, they might add: "You are just more single-minded on analyzing the patient–therapist interaction, while we are more flexible and eclectic."

I have two sources of skepticism over such a stance. One source is my own experience of listening to other psychotherapists talking and writing about their work, and of supervising psychotherapy. The other source is more theoretical in nature.

First, let me say something about my experience as a psychotherapist (I am also a psychoanalyst). I trained at the Maudsley Hospital, London, where I became a Consultant Psychiatrist in Psychotherapy, and then in 1991 I moved to the Adult Department of the Tavistock Clinic, London. Even in these settings, where it was customary for trainees to conduct individual psychodynamic psychotherapy for between nine months and two or three years, there was substantial variation in quite how therapists worked in the transference. It was certainly not the case that all psychotherapy involved a particular set of techniques, because therapists approached their work in different ways. If this variability was the norm in these privileged psychodynamic settings, then how much more variability is to be expected among dynamic psychotherapists elsewhere. From my somewhat limited experience of supervising beyond London, I believe such variations in practice are huge. I am sure they are even more marked when therapists are not even *trying* to analyze the transference.

Then there is my theoretical concern, which pivots about the question, "How similar is similar?" It is not just that therapists mean very different things when they talk of recognizing and interpreting the transference (see Hobson and Kapur 2005 for an empirical study). For Brief Psychoanalytic Therapy, so much depends upon the therapist's immersion in a specific kind of relation with the patient. The therapist needs to sustain a particular mode as well as focus of attentiveness to what is happening in the therapeutic encounter. Even *if* one or more ingredients of another approach have surface similarity to what goes on in Brief Psychoanalytic Therapy, the nature and significance of such elements can be radically altered by *other* modes of therapeutic orientation and engagement with which the business of analyzing the transference is admixed. This is over and beyond the effects of diluting the therapist's commitment to tracking qualities of shifting patient–therapist relatedness.

So if someone were to dismiss the specialness of Brief Psychoanalytic Therapy on the basis that similar transference-based interpretative work can occur in a therapy that involves explicitly educational procedures or joint problem solving, I would weigh that argument carefully. I do wonder whether eclectic approaches that combine various technical strategies are different creatures altogether. I struggle to imagine how a thoroughgoing focus on the transference is compatible with the therapist engaging in a lot of other, non-transferentially based activities such as dwelling on the patient's history of attachments, suggesting alternative ways to manage relationships or to resolve conflicting feelings, or myriad other styles of non-analytic intervention. If talking *about* the patient's condition occupies centre-stage, as so often it does in psychotherapies, surely it must be difficult to achieve the kind of on-the-ball, often interwoven and successively elaborated interpretive interventions illustrated throughout this book.

On the other hand, of course, there are criticisms that might be levelled at the "less is more" approach that characterizes the relatively restricted orientation of Brief Psychoanalytic Therapy. Readers may recall that in Chapter 2, I expressed my view that an excerpt of therapy transcript recorded by Lemma, Target, and Fonagy (2011) was a good illustration of the kind of working in the transference that Brief Psychoanalytic Therapy also advocates. At the end of the day, it remains an open question whether the other procedures and attitudes that characterize Dynamic Interpersonal Therapy enhance or detract from the effects of such transference-based work. Brief Psychoanalytic Therapy may be effective in promoting certain kinds of therapeutic development, but there might be a risk of sacrificing flexibility and withholding complementary avenues of interpersonal exploration that benefit at least some patients.

One question that arises here is what contributes to or detracts from depth in patient–therapist communication. What does it take to make deep interpersonal contact, and why does it matter?

Depth of communication, and the process of change

What does it mean to communicate in depth, and what are the obstacles to such communication, whether between persons or within an individual's own mind? These are central questions for psychodynamic psychotherapy. A primary aim of psychotherapy is to facilitate both interpersonal and intrapsychic communication and to heal splits in the personality. These are the means to lessen suffering or emotional restriction and promote health and fulfilment.

Of course, all kinds of anxiety or conflict, and all kinds of deviation or deficit, can contribute both to depth of contact, and its limitation. In some patients, barriers to deeper engagement are *relatively* straightforward to discern and address, and here, psychotherapeutic intervention seems to release momentum toward renewed development. In other, more troubled patients, where interpersonal experience is more threatening and hostile and splits in the person's personality more severe, progress can be much more choppy and labored.

A principal difference among psychotherapies is how the means to change is conceptualized. Many would include insight in their list of therapeutic factors, at least insofar as a patient is enabled to think about him or herself in new ways. Most would consider it valuable when a patient is able to experience, express, and integrate previously disowned elements of his or her mental life. Beyond that, however, one can see there is a much stronger teaching/educational element in some approaches, whereas others focus on the transformational and integrative power of a therapist registering and articulating current emotionally laden interpersonal transactions.

Let me say a little more about Brief Psychoanalytic Therapy in this respect. To rehearse what I have written previously, the fundamental principle is that change in the individual (intrapsychic) is promoted by change in the individual's experience of self-in-relation-to-other (interpersonal). One way such change has been conceptualized (Bion 1967) is in terms of the patient owning what has, up to now, been projected into others. In other words, one way of disowning one's own attitudes and states of mind is to attribute these to someone else, and, not infrequently, to evoke corresponding attitudes and states of mind in the other person. A therapist's capacity to register and contain what is projected affects a patient's ability to re-integrate what has been split off and ejected from where it belongs within the personality.

There are always reasons why a person projects or otherwise limits awareness of aspects of his or her emotional life. Often the reasons have to do with negative feelings such as those of anguish, fear, hatred, destructiveness, envy, and so on, which have their source in intimate relationships, past and present. If someone deals with such feelings by projecting them into other people and encountering the projected attitudes as coming from outside and not from within, or by otherwise repressing or splitting them off from consciousness so they are unavailable for integration, then a price to be paid is in depth of experience. This applies to the psychotherapeutic relationship, as to any other. If one is trying to facilitate depth in a patient's interpersonal engagement and awareness of self, then it is likely that the patient's negative and destructive attitudes are going to be very important. This being so, and given that the most alive and immediate instance of relatedness available in psychotherapy is that between patient and therapist, then the therapist needs to make manifest and deal with such negative feelings in the transference.

If one adopts this kind of perspective—and there is no compulsion to do so—then one can ask how far each form of psychotherapy creates conditions in which negative and disturbed as well as positive and more integrated feelings toward the therapist become manifest to be addressed in the present as well as recognized in the abstract, that is, contained in the therapeutic relationship as well as discussed as an important topic. Although one might question the relative non-directive stance of the Brief Psychoanalytic therapist and his or her inclination to pick up a patient's hostile or evasive attitudes *as well as* the patient's anxieties and vulnerabilities, it is by no means the case that this approach needs to be blaming or persecuting. As I have stated before, if a therapist can recognize and address negative feelings, then often the patient feels relieved. This is a vital part of psychotherapy. Not infrequently, it is needed if depth in communication, and through this, movement toward integration and health, is to be achieved.

Specialness reconsidered

So much for distinctiveness in the qualities of Brief Psychoanalytic Therapy. There is a quite different question, whether the specialness of the approach really matters for the effectiveness of treatment. I will take up just two of the many facets of this further question.

Firstly, there are those who take the view, sometimes with more than a hint of cynicism, that all therapies work primarily through factors that are not specific to particular therapies. At the end of the day, they suggest, it doesn't matter too much what goes on in therapy, within pretty wide limits. I find this so startling a suggestion, I hardly know what to say. I am reminded of a colleague, who when considering the matter, reflected: "Is classical music the same as jazz?"

Picture yourself entering Brief Psychoanalyic Therapy and having an experience akin to that of any one of the patients described in this book. Now imagine that what you encountered instead was a therapist who felt his or her primary task was to provide unconditional positive regard and empathy, or one whose principal concern was to adjust your negative cognitions, or one whose intent was to explore your attachment history. Or come to that, imagine a therapist who ascribed all kinds of meanings to your behavior, with little or no substantiating evidence to support interpretations. It is difficult to make this point without caricature, but it seems wildly implausible that a supportive relationship (for example) is more or less all that matters. Was it not convincing that for the patients described in this book, the therapeutic work addressed person-specific issues for which there was explicit evidence, and which the patients as well as the therapists considered to be of vital significance for their lives?

A second, more complex matter concerns intrinsic variability among therapists. The idea here is that, whether or not one treatment differs from another, such differences are swamped by "therapist effects." Some therapists appear to be substantially more effective than others, within any given treatment approach. One implication is that it may matter more whom a patient sees than the therapeutic approach adopted by the therapist.

I acknowledge that there is something important in this argument, and I would be willing to hazard some guesses as to qualities present in good therapists, and lacking in those who are less good (try this: a therapist's capacities to listen deeply, and to manage and reflect on his or her own emotional responses). What I find questionable is whether such factors mean that the treatment approach hardly matters. I am very willing to accept that Brief Psychoanalytic Therapy could be worse than useless in the wrong therapist's hands—I have written harsh words about technique without heart—but I do not think it follows that the approach is not *special in the right hands*. I doubt whether it is the case that an able therapist working in this way would promote the same developments with the same patients as, say, an able CAT therapist, but I admit the matter is open. I am on firmer ground in believing that different approaches suit different patients, and I know for a fact that Brief Psychoanalytic Therapy is not appropriate for everyone.

I shall conclude this discussion of specialness on a personal note. In Chapter 2, I discussed the Conversational Model devised by my father Bob Hobson, and developed and studied as Psychodynamic Interpersonal Therapy by an impressive and loyal group of clinicians including Russell Meares, Frank Margison, Elspeth Guthrie, David Shapiro, and Michael Barkham (Barkham et al. 2016; Guthrie 1999). I am well aware of my indebtedness to my father's ideas. It does not take a Sherlock Holmes to notice the family resemblance between tenets of the Conversational Model (Chapter 2) and certain items of the BPT Adherence Scale. On the other hand, the treatments have important differences in style and emphasis. For example, a central and original feature of the Conversational Model is its particular approach to augmenting a patient's expression and communication of feelings. This contrasts with the manner in which a therapist engaged in Brief Psychoanalytic Therapy tracks patient–therapist relatedness in its moment-by-moment vicissitudes.

I am deeply impressed with the versatility of the Conversational Model, and how it has been used as a means to launch health service workers of various professional groups into conducting psychodynamic psychotherapy. Once embarked on such work, therapists can and will learn on the job. Whereas Brief Psychoanalytic Therapy is unfitted for beginners, it too has a "learn on the job" dimension. Like the Conversational Model, its principles may be applied without a swathe of theoretical/conceptual commitments, even though, all being well, a practitioner will be led to draw on psychoanalytic theory. I do wonder whether there is a potential fit between the two approaches, as therapists who are so inclined follow a developmental trajectory from the Conversational Model to Brief Psychoanalytic Therapy, or move in the other direction and enrich or modify Brief Psychoanalytic Therapy by assimilating ideas and techniques from the Conversational Model. But perhaps, given the family connection, that is wishful thinking.

Concluding remarks

There we have it. Brief Psychoanalytic Therapy is brief, to be sure; and at least arguably, it is psychoanalytic, especially insofar as it encourages a sustained focus on the transference. This form of psychotherapy should allow—indeed, propel—a practitioner to draw on profound insights that psychoanalysis affords, as well as to benefit from the kind of in-depth supervision that is so much a part of psychoanalytic practice. In my view, psychotherapy fashioned according to the principles outlined here attains something of the depth inherent in psychoanalytic work. And at least sometimes, it has the potential to expand, even transform, patients' emotional lives.

References

Abbass, A.A., Kisely, S.R., Town, J.M., et al. (2014). Short-term psychodynamic psychotherapies for common mental disorders (Review). *The Cochrane Library*, Issue 7.

Barkham, M., Guthrie, E., Hardy, G.E., & Margison, F. (2016). *Psychodynamic-interpersonal therapy: A conversational model*. In press, Sage.

Bion, W.R. (1959). Attacks on linking. *International Journal of Psycho-Analysis*, *40*, 308–315

Bion, W.R. (1962a). A theory of thinking. *International Journal of Psycho-Analysis*, *43*, 306–310.

Bion, W.R. (1962b). *Learning from Experience*. London: Heinemann (reprinted London: Karnac Books, 1984).

Bion, W.R. (1967). *Second Thoughts*. London: Karnac.

Bion, W.R. (1988, originally 1967). Notes on memory and desire. In E.B. Spillius (ed.), *Melanie Klein Today, Vol 2*, pp 17–21. London: Routledge.

Bollas, C. (1992). The psychoanalyst's use of free association. In *Being a Character*, pp. 101–133. Hove: Routledge.

Botella, C. and Botella, S. (2005). *The Work of Psychic Figurability*. Hove and New York: Brunner-Routledge.

Britton, R. (1998). *Belief and Imagination*. London: Routledge.

Britton, R., Feldman, M., and O'Shaughnessy, E. (eds) (1989). *The Oedipus Complex Today*. London: Karnac.

Butler, S.F., Henry, W.P., and Strupp, H.H. (1995). Measuring adherence in time- limited dynamic psychotherapy. *Psychotherapy: Theory, Research, Practice, Training*, *32*, 629–638.

Coltart, N. (1992, originally 1985). *Slouching towards Bethlehem*. London: Free Association Books.

Davanloo, H. (1994, originally 1978). *Basic Principles and Techniques in Short-Term Psychotherapy*. Northvale, NJ: Aronson.

Denman, C. (2001). Cognitive-analytic therapy. *Advances in Psychiatric Treatment*, *7*, 243–252.

Eliot, T.S. (1969, originally 1917). The love song of J. Alfred Prufrock. In *The Complete Poems and Plays of T.S. Eliot*. London: Faber.

Eysenck. H. (1985) *Decline and Fall of the Freudian Empire*. New York: Viking Penguin.

Fairbairn, W.R.D. (1952). *Psychoanalytic Studies of the Personality*. London: Tavistock; New York: Basic Books.

Feldman, M. (1997). Projective identification: the analyst's involvement. *International Journal of Psycho-Analysis*, *78*, 227–241.

Feldman, M. (2009). The illumination of history. In B. Joseph (ed.), *Doubt, Conviction, and the Analytic Process: Selected Papers of Michael Feldman*, pp. 72–95. London: Routledge.

Fonagy, P. (2001). *Attachment Theory and Psychoanalysis*. New York: Other Press.

Fonagy, P., Rost, F., Carlyle, J-A, et al. (2015). Pragmatic randomized controlled trial of long-term psychoanalytic psychotherapy for treatment-resistant depression: the Tavistock Adult Depression Study (TADS). *World Psychiatry*, *14*, 312–321.

Freud, S. (1900). *The Interpretation of Dreams*. In J. Strachey (ed.), *Standard Edition of the Complete Psychological Works of Sigmund Freud*, Vols 4 and 5. London: Hogarth.

Freud, S. (1905). Fragment of an analysis of a case of hysteria. In J. Strachey (ed.), *Standard Edition of the Complete Psychological Works of Sigmund Freud*, Vol. 7, pp. 7–122. London: Hogarth

Freud, S. (1912). The dynamics of transference. In J. Strachey (ed.), *Standard Edition of the Complete Psychological Works of Sigmund Freud*, Vol. 12, pp. 97–108. London: Hogarth.

Freud, S. (1915). The unconscious. In J. Strachey (ed.), *Standard Edition of the Complete Psychological Works of Sigmund Freud*, Vol. 14, pp. 166–215. London: Hogarth.

Freud, S. (1917). Mourning and melancholia. In J. Strachey (ed.), *Standard Edition of the Complete Psychological Works of Sigmund Freud*, Vol. 14, pp. 237–258. London: Hogarth.

Freud, S. (1923). Two encyclopaedia articles: (A) Psycho-analysis. In J. Strachey (ed.), *Standard Edition of the Complete Psychological Works of Sigmund Freud*, Vol 18, pp. 235–254.

Gerber, A.J., Kocsis, J.H., Milrod, B.L., et al. (2011). A quality-based review of randomized controlled trials of psychodynamic psychotherapy. *American Journal of Psychiatry*, *168*, 19–28.

Guthrie, E. (1999). Psychodynamic Interpersonal Therapy. *Advances in Psychiatric Treatment*, *5*, 135–145.

Guthrie, E., Moorey, J., Margison, et al. (1999). Cost-effectiveness of brief psychodynamic-interpersonal therapy in high utilizers of psychiatric services. *Archives of General Psychiatry*, *56*, 519–526.

Hamlyn, D.W. (1974). Person-perception and our understanding of others. In T. Mischel (ed.), *Understanding Other Persons*, pp. 1–36. Oxford: Blackwell.

Heimann, P. (1950). On counter-transference. *International Journal of Psycho-Analysis*, *31*, 81–84.

Hobson, R.F. (1985). *Forms of Feeling*. London: Tavistock.

Hobson, R.P. (1993). The emotional origins of social understanding. *Philosophical Psychology*, *6*, 227–249.

Hobson R.P. (2002/2004). *The Cradle of Thought*. London: Macmillan (and 2004: New York, Oxford University Press).

Hobson, R.P. (2008). Self-representing dreams. *Psychoanalytic Psychotherapy*, *22*, 20–30. Originally published in the journal in 1985, and reprinted for a Special Issue.

Hobson, R.P. (ed.) (2013). *Consultations in Psychoanalytic Psychotherapy*. London: Karnac.

Hobson, R.P. (2014). The making of mind. *Psychoanalytic Inquiry*, *34*, 817–830.

Hobson, R.P. and Kapur, R. (2005). Working in the transference: clinical and research perspectives. *Psychology & Psychotherapy: Theory, Research and Practice*, *78*, 1–21.

Hobson, R.P., Patrick, M.P.H., and Valentine, J.D. (1998). Objectivity in psychoanalytic judgements. *British Journal of Psychiatry*, *173*, 172–177.

Hobson, R.P., Patrick, M., Kapur, R., and Lyons-Ruth, K. (2013). Research reflections. In R.P. Hobson (ed.), *Consultations in Psychoanalytic Psychotherapy*, pp. 183–203. London: Karnac.

Holmes, J. (1993). Attachment theory: A biological basis for psychotherapy? *British Journal of Psychiatry, 163*, 430–438.

Isaacs, S. (1948). The nature and function of phantasy. *International Journal of Psycho-Analysis, 29*, 73–97.

Joseph, B. (1989*). Psychic Equilibrium and Psychic Change*. London: Tavistock/Routledge.

Klein, M. (1975a, originally 1946). Notes on some schizoid mechanisms. In *Envy and Gratitude and Other Works 1946–1963*, pp. 1–24. London: Hogarth.

Klein, M. (1975b, originally 1957). Envy and gratitude. In *Envy and Gratitude and Other Works 1946–1963*, pp. 176–235. London: Hogarth.

Leichsenring, F. (2005). Are psychodynamic and psychoanalytic therapies effective? A review of empirical data. *International Journal of Psychoanalysis, 86*, 841–868.

Leichsenring, F., Rabung, S., and Leibing E. (2004). The efficacy of short-term psychodynamic psychotherapy in specific psychiatric disorders: a meta-analysis. *Archives of General Psychiatry, 61*, 1208–1216.

Lemma, A., Target, M., and Fonagy, P. (2010). The development of a brief psychodynamic protocol for depression: Dynamic Interpersonal Therapy (DIT). *Psychoanalytic Psychotherapy, 24*, 329–346.

Lemma, A., Target, M., and Fonagy, P. (2011). *Brief Dynamic Interpersonal Therapy*. Oxford: Oxford University Press.

Levine, H.B. (2012). The colourless canvas: representation, therapeutic action and the creation of mind. *International Journal of Psychoanalysis, 93*, 606–629.

Malan, D. and Della Silva, P.C. (2006). *Lives Transformed*. London: Karnac.

Milrod, B., Leon, A.C., Busch, F., et al. (2007). A randomized controlled clinical trial of psychoanalytic psychotherapy for panic disorder. *American Journal of Psychiatry, 164*, 265–272.

Ogden, T.H. (1986). *The Matrix of the Mind*. London: Karnac.

Ogden, T.H. (1994). *Subjects of Analysis*. London: Karnac.

Ogden, T.H. (2002). A new reading of the origins of object-relations theory. *International Journal of Psycho-Analysis, 83*, 767–782.

Ogrodniczuk, J.S. and Piper, W.E. (1999). Measuring therapist technique in psychodynamic psychotherapies. *Journal of Psychotherapy Practice and Research, 8*, 142–154.

O'Shaughnessy, E. (1988, originally 1981). A clinical study of a defensive organization. In E.B. Spillius (ed.), *Melanie Klein Today, Vol. 1: Mainly Theory*, pp. 293–310. London: Routledge.

Perelberg, R.J. (ed.) (2000). *Dreaming and Thinking*. London: Karnac.

Racker, H. (1968). *Transference and Countertransference*. Croydon: Maresfield Reprints.

Riesenberg-Malcolm, R. (1995). The three "W"s: what, where and when: the rationale of interpretation. *International Journal of Psycho-Analysis, 76*, 447–456.

Rosenfeld, H. (1971). A clinical approach to the psychoanalytic theory of the life and death instincts: an investigation into the aggressive aspects of narcissism. *International Journal of Psycho-Analysis, 52*, 169–178.

Rosenfeld, H. (1988, originally 1971). Contribution to the psychopathology of psychotic states: the importance of projective identification in the ego structure and the object relations of the psychotic patient. In E. Spillius (ed.), *Melanie Klein Today, Vol. 1: Mainly Theory*, pp. 117–137. London: Routledge.

Roth, P. (2001). Mapping the landscape: Levels of transference interpretation. *International Journal of Psycho-Analysis*, *82*, 533–543.

Rycroft, C. (1956/1968). Symbolism and its relationship to the primary and secondary process. In *Imagination and Reality*, pp. 42–60. London: Hogarth.

Ryle, A. and Kerr, I.B. (2002). *Introducing Cognitive Analytic Therapy*. Chichester: Wiley.

Safran, J.D. (2002). Brief Relational Psychoanalytic Treatment. *Psychoanalytic Dialogues*, *12*, 171–195.

Sandler, J. (1976). Countertransference and role-responsiveness. *International Review of Psycho-Analysis*, *3*, 43–47.

Sandler, J. and Rosenblatt, B. (1987, originally 1962). The representational world. In J. Sandler (ed.), *From Safety to Superego*, pp. 58–72. London: Karnac.

Segal, H. (1981). The function of dreams. In *The Work of Hanna Segal: A Kleinian Approach to Clinical Practice*, pp. 89–97. New York: Jason Aronson.

Spillius, E. and O'Shaughnessy, E. (2012). *Projective Identification: The Fate of a Concept*. London: Routledge.

Steiner, J. (1993). *Psychic Retreats. Pathological Organizations in Psychotic, Neurotic and Borderline Patients*. London: Routledge.

Strachey, J. (1934). The nature of the therapeutic action of psychoanalysis. *International Journal of Psycho-Analysis*, *15*, 127–159.

Strupp, H.H. and Binder, J. (1984). *Psychotherapy in a New Key: A Guide to Time-Limited Dynamic Psychotherapy*. New York: Basic.

Stuart, S. (2009). IPT Adherence and Quality Scale. Unpublished manuscript, Interpersonal Psychotherapy Institute, Iowa.

Taylor, D. (2015). Treatment manuals and the advancement of psychoanalytic knowledge: the Treatment Manual of the Tavistock Adult Depression Study. *International Journal of Psychoanalysis*, *96*, 845–875.

Vygotsky, L.S. (1978). Internalization of higher psychological functions. In M. Cole, V. John-Steiner, S. Scribner, and E. Souberman (eds.), *Mind in Society: The Development of Higher Psychological Processes*, pp. 52–57. Cambridge, MA: Harvard University Press.

Waddington, C.H. (1977). *Tools for Thought*. London: Paladin.

Weissman, M.M., Markowitz, J.C., and Klerman, G.L. (2007). *Clinician's Quick Guide to Interpersonal Psychotherapy*. Oxford: Oxford University Press.

Winnicott, D.W. (1965a, originally 1963). The development of the capacity for concern. In *The Maturational Processes and the Facilitating Environment*, pp. 73–82. London: Hogarth.

Winnicott, D.W. (1965b, originally 1960). The theory of the parent–infant relationship. In *The Maturational Processes and the Facilitating Environment*, pp. 37–55. London: Hogarth.

Wollheim, R. (1969). The mind and the mind's image of itself. *International Journal of Psycho-Analysis*, *50*, 209–220.

Index